Q++ and a Non-Standard Model

 www.trafford.com

North America & international
toll-free: 844-688-6899 (USA & Canada)
fax: 812 355 4082

Q++ and a Non-Standard Model

The *Digital World Theory* Version 2.0 :
Quantum Programming Language and Implementation
Considerations

Lucian Miti Ionescu

A Mathematical-Physics and Computer Science
Unifying Approach
VI ReQuEST

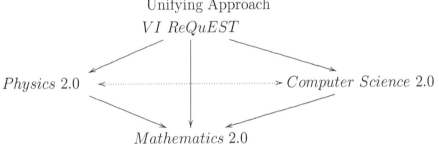

Physics 2.0   *Computer Science* 2.0

Mathematics 2.0

The MPCS-Alliance

To Daniela

Panta Rei

Contents

Preface

Quantum Physics is *Quantum Information Processing*, represents a two-ways Turing-Church-Deutsch principle. We therefore need a quantum computing language, Q++, to model and design "reality": the *Quantum Software* and *Quantum Hardware*.

The elementary quantum computing gates, as a basic instruction set, are the "elementary" particles and the corresponding "fundamental" interactions, except that, from an information processing point of view there is only *one*: **the qubit**, with its dual functions of data and program! Its "external manifestation" is the electron, with its "internal counterpart", the quark; Fermi's neutrino solution to the balance of momentum and energy is (hopefully) replaced by duality.

In this book, some non-conventional ideas are *explored away* from the traditional *Standard Model*, as part of the *Digital World Theory Project*.

For example, we suggest interpreting a three-dimensional time and space symmetry as a quark color current (internal magnetic charges), in an "external-internal" supersymmetric electro-magnetism (IE-duality of the Hodge-de Rham Quantum Dot Resolution), unifying QED and QCD, with the weak interactions coming as a byproduct.

Gravity is expected to emerge as an entropic organizational principle, to get a part of the complexified action.

At the mathematical implementation level, "the quark" is just a primitive element corresponding to prime numbers under the cyclotomic representation of the universal Hopf ring: integers with multiplication and divisibility (comultiplication). *Divisibility* is the correct concept in the non-commutative world; **not** *fields of fractions*, but rather *Hopf Objects!*

The "Ultimate Particle-Physics Theory" is *Number Theory*: *Galois Theory* with *Klein's Program* as a geometric classification interpretation, dressed up in the language of homological and homotopical algebra.

Q++ models not only the "mother of all quantum phenomena", as Feynman once put it, but also the "father": the *Quantum Erasure* experiment.

But the most striking feature presented here, is the underlying *Simplified Picture* of the elementary physics. There is "no motion" in the classical sense; all is *teleportation* at the speed of light in the quantum fluctuating network representing the causal structure, whether it is an internal quantum state or an external classical state like momentum. This allows to permanently get rid of "void ambient space-time", classical or quantum ("vacuum").

The gain is considerable: special relativity *and* quantum theory are thus implemented with one stroke as a *Quantum Information Flow* in a *Dynamic Network* [1].

Other "brainstorming" considerations include: a framework for *Quantum Gravity*, what are mass and entropy, how quantum erasure is eavesdropping on a quantum communication etc.

---

[1]Quantum space-time fluctuations can be compared with reconfigurations of the neuron network of the cortex.

The book contains enough inciting ideas for both the layman as well as for the specialist. For the mathematician and his/her graduate students we mention: why *fields* should be replaced by *bifields* (Hopf objects), as part of the categorification of mathematics (not only of physics!), how the commutative determinant can be generalized as the Feynman Path Integral etc.

It also contains enough motivation, I believe, to incite the physicist to "reprogram" some old applications: the particle-antiparticle dichotomy is a time-orientation/ information flow issue; the $SU_2 \times$ *generations* (only three?) assumes a grand unifying group extension, while we suggest an infinite basis of Lie elements (primes); how mass can be regarded as a Galois index, consistent with the idea that mass is generated by breaking the symmetry (Higgs mechanism) etc.

More importantly, I invite the reader to look for some new possibilities: nonconventional transportation [2], quantum computers and quantum gravity computers etc.

The DWT series, from which this is the second book, has the role of "webstorming" an open source science project. I hope you will be part of it.

Limits are confined to mathematics.

---

[2]If "everything" is teleportation, why are we spending so much in technologies increasing the temperature-entropy?

CHAPTER 1

Introduction

$Q + +$ is a systematic assimilation of the main concepts in quantum mathematics and physics, organized around a kernel of ideas and principles stated as the DWT. There is no need to "rewrite" the "old applications" in the new language, except for selected cases for testing purposes and to gain "fluency" with the new language.

The crucial exciting new application is quantum gravity *within the framework of the SM*: quarks and electrons (three generations). One big question is: "Can we dispose of the "weak force" as being merely the IE-duality?".

Mathematically speaking, a good principle to follow in this rewriting physics and mathematics enterprise is: "Forget fields; rethink them as Hopf objects!".

The main advantage of implementing the DWT, as a conceptual framework / interface to quantum physics, in Q++ (QDR etc.) is that the implementation is already a quantum theory with no need for quantization nor renormalization, being from the start "computer friendly".

The presentation has often the style of a "traveling diary": what-I-see-is-what-you-get, with no time for a detailed analysis. Instead, I set forth my personal interpretation together with my conviction that the many interesting places visited will brainstorm the reader. There are plenty of research problems suggested, as part of the development of the DWT, which could interest both the expert and the graduate student.

In a pictorial sense, Feynman helped *Quantum Physics* (QP) and *Quantum Computing* (QC) get to know each other. Soon after that the developments in quantum computing (Deutsch etc.) led to an "engagement". The DWT project [24] advocates the permanence and benefits of this two way conceptual bridge.

In this essay we suggest various "non-standard" ideas to be explored in order to design a new "operating system for the quantum reality" [1]. As stated by many already, there is a need for a radical change at the level of the foundations of science. We believe that there is nothing wrong with the technical tools developed so far in mathematical-physics, from the point of view of their functionality; what has to be changed is the mathematical-material used to develop them, which in turn has to be supported by a shift in our conceptual understanding. This can be done if the corresponding physics interpretation benefits from the computer science experience.

1. A Generalized *Equivalence Principle*

We start from the above "marriage" between quantum physics and computer science, which naturally leads, at a philosophical level, to a new fundamental *Equivalence Principle* completing the unification of mater-energy and space-time started and developed over 35 years by Einstein. To his unification we add the aspects pertaining to *quantum information*, with its mandatory changes: since matter and energy are quantized, and so is information (qubits), space-time *and* "*motion*" must be quantized too ([**23, 28, 39**] etc.).

---

[1]Rewriting the *Standard Model* in $Q + +$.

The new *Energy-matter-space-time-information Equiv-alence Principle* suggested in [**23**] is mandated by the general trend in the development of today's physics. It is also suggested by the evolution of the mathematical models and methods, notably the use of graphs-categories-networks (automata) in modeling *complex systems of interacting subsystems.*

We will present in this section only an "update"; for previous developments of the search for a new fundamental principle see [**18, 23, 24, 28**].

At a rigorous mathematical-physics level, the implementation is based on tools belonging to homological algebra, including an algebraic framework for the *Feynman Path Integral* [**35, 19, 22, 21, 25, 26**]. The underlying idea is an algebraic version of *Multi-Resolution Analysis* (MRA), e.g. Haar wavelets (or MapQuest.com!): resolving the phenomenology of a system as a homological algebra resolution of subsystems and interactions called the *Quantum Dot Resolution* [**24**]. It "balances" internal and external degrees of freedom (I/E DOFs), via a duality [**33**] [2]. The "external DOF part" is in some sense "classical" ("space-time", if the causal structure admits one such structure), while the "internal DOF part" is "quantum" (quantum numbers as DOFs).

The added feature, due to the merger with information (quantum computing perspective), is that entropy H, as a measure of symmetry, is part of the action.

Given Γ a "transition path" with its corresponding symmetry in the spirit of a Galois-Klein correspondence, then

$$H = \ln|Aut(\Gamma)|, \quad \mathcal{S} = S + i\hbar H.$$

$$K(I,O) = \int_{Hom(I,O)} \mathcal{D}\Gamma \; e^{i\mathcal{S}/\hbar}.$$

---

[2]It is typical of other dualities: Fourier, Pontrjagin, Poincare and Tannaka-Krein.

Feynman Path Integral (FPI) of the second equation is the crowning of the Lagrangian approach to modern semi-classical physics, while the first equation is a core addition of the DWT, with its categorical implementation of the FPI in the spirit of today's discrete models (simplicial models, Spin Networks and Foams, Loop Quantum Gravity, Lattice Gauge Theory etc.).

General Relativity	Energy-Matter Space-Time	Entropy-Information Symmetry	DWT

For additional explanations, see [28] (update of [23]).

The conceptual implications of such an equivalence principle (super-symmetry), implemented as the *IE-duality* , include trading space-time (EDOFs) for matter/mass (IDOF) and quantizing "everything": energy, matter, space and time, together with information.

The external observable properties of an interaction (external level) are modeled using a network/Feynman graph/Riemann surface as an element of the *Causal Structure* which is implemented mathematically as a *Feynman Category* . If such an *interaction mode* admits a *space-time coordinate system* , then "Space", thought of as "parallel computing", can be traded for "Time", thought of as sequential computing. At the internal level ("conjugate variables") this "trading-duality" corresponds to a *generalized Wick rotation* :

$$\mathcal{E} = ic\mathcal{P}, \quad \mathcal{E} = E + ik_b H, \quad \mathcal{P} = p + ic\, m_0.$$
$$(1.1)$$

Therefore **NOT** space is in need of additional dimensions (e.g. "classical" String Theory), but we need to "blow-up" the "abelian time" to a 3-dimensional non-abelian time (qubit/symmetry flow: $SU(2)$).

2. Newton or Democrit?

"Continuum or Discrete?"; this is the question!

The main "mathematics-material" for building classical physics was (and still is) the *real numbers*, which are not so real after all; complex numbers fit better a complex reality!

On the other hand physics theories, no matter how elegant in their "continuum dress" made out of the concept of manifold as a raw material, ultimately needs to be *discretized* in order to take advantage of the computational power of computer simulations, classical or quantum (Lattice Gauge Theory etc.) [3].

The main steps in the development of physics consisted in steps leading to further quantization, and abandoning the continuum point of view: Plank and energy quanta, Einstein and photons, de Broglie and particle-wave duality, Feynman and every QFT-interaction etc.

I emphasized in [18] that all we need in order to model the evolution of a dynamical system is a "class of paths" thought of as transitions, and implemented algebraically [4]. Later the idea became technically clear: *Feynman Categories* and *Feynman Processes* [25, 26].

The Feynman approach was, and still is looked upon as an approximation scheme. I pointed out that it can be interpreted as a "resolution approach"; then it is "exact" and NOT an approximation, for the same reasons we can replace and object by its resolution [12, 24, 25]. For example a group can be presented as a quotient of a free group by a set of relations; the free group may be thought of as the "linear approximation", while the next level of approximation gives the object itself: the group.

---

[3]... and topology may lead to "hard analysis"!

[4]The categorical analog of the maximal ideal which in algebraic geometry replaces the "point" of a space-time.

"Approximations" are models like Lattice Gauge Theory, Loop Quantum Gravity etc., which *fix a level of approximation* while the (classical) object, say space-time is obtained as a continuum limit, e.g. when the lattice size tends to zero. There is no guarantee that the "dual limit" is still classical or it exists altogether. Nevertheless such theories are needed for computational purposes, and in fact are quite successful.

3. Methodology: Top-Down Design

Therefore, *regardless* of the particular reasons of one group of scientists or another, we **need** *discrete models of finite type*; other examples are the Feynman-Kontsevich graphs and our *Quantum Dot Resolution* (QDR) [24] etc. It has the advantage of being an algebraic approach, i.e. axiomatic, compatible with a top-down design methodology, in contrast with Newton-Leibnitz analysis (bottom-up methodology, constructive), or even Poincare's topology ("in between", qualitative yet with a lot of "pathologies"). MacLane's category theory comes as the perfect object-and-relations oriented language for this purpose, where geometry and physics come with the needed "intuition" on top of its often mentioned "abstract non-sense" attribute.

We reinforce the idea that the answer/solution, irrespective of the particular motivation, is, in my opinion: *The mathematical model of a (modern) quantum theory should be discrete of finite type* , i.e. finite dimensional in each integer degree, *designed top-down from an algebraic-axiomatic interface binded to the physics application*, like geometry.

4. *The* Standard Model or *a* Quantum Programming Language?

In this article we push further the correlation between quantum physics (QP) and quantum computing

(QC), including aspects from the methodology of the later. We aim to present the elementary particle theory as an "object-oriented" language, designed for programming reality (physics experimental setup: quantum hardware, and theoretical model: quantum software).

Our concern is *not* a "Theory of Everything" [5], but the design of *a* language modeling the complex reality. It will evolve and then be superceded by a better one in the cyclical cycle of research. We therefore are *not* interested in the "mathematical exception" we rather view as a "pathological situation" (E_8, Monster group etc.), but rather in the generic, flexible and upgradable mathematical "materials and technologies".

The present exploratory alternative to the *Standard Model* is motivated by the mandatory changes in our understanding of what space-time-matter really are. The "technical implementation", more or less viable, is only hinted, due to lack of time and expertise of the present author, and it is intended first for exemplification purposes. An important point is that the technical tools are *already developed* (Standard Model, String Theory, Loop Quantum Gravity, Lattice Gauge Theory etc.), yet they are "written" in the "old classical language": all we have to do is to rewrite the code in Q++!

This explains the style of the exposition, i.e. that of a research report: second phase of the *DWT-project* [**24**]. We "put the cards on the table", since the Linux open source development project showed that the WWW is the "perfect collaborator"! The analogy goes even further; as in any top-down design of an informational system, we design the interface first, represented by names in italics, for which the implementation is just a matter of ... time or energy. And the Web is the interface to many more skillful mathematics-physics specialists capable of compiling the present authors speculations from

---

[5]Like "the set of all sets", it leads to "trouble".

the high level language into solid mathematical-physics code. Then what remains is a "link-editing" with the current theories, to get a computational viable theory ("executable code").

The reader probably agrees that the era of a one-person's breakthrough-theory ended, perhaps with Einstein, and projects like the DWT-Project are suited for a collective effort.

CHAPTER 2

Modeling Particle Physics

In view of the QP/QC correspondence, to design a model (application) for particle physics, we need to settle for a suitable *quantum programming language* : $Q++$. It is essentially a quantum computing perspective on the elementary particle physics: particles are *quantum registers* of various "data types" (irreducible representations), interaction vertices are *quantum gates* etc. The fundamental interactions, instead of being modeled as "force fields" in a Newtonian view of a continuum space-time, in the discrete finite-type model (DWT/QDR) they are modeled as *elementary gates* : the "basic instruction set" the universe as a quantum computer uses.

1. Why THREE!

Beyond the language issue (FORTRAN or C++, a skillful programmer can do well with both!), there are some deep questions, collectively referred to by "Why THREE?": space-time dimensions (because of the rotational symmetry $SO(3)$; but why 3?), three generations of particles, three colors for QCD etc. [1]

We will explore a non-standard approach, building the *physics interface* of particle physics on the QDR model. We start (in a brain-storming way) from the two "sides of reality", *external DOFs* (causality structure , momentum-position etc.) and *internal DOFs* (quantum numbers etc.) in duality:

---

[1] A laconic answer is: because TWO is "commutative"!

	External Space	Duality	Internal Space
Fermions	Electron	Neutrino	Quark
Bosons	Photon	Graviton	Gluon
Data type	$R^{3\times2}$	$\otimes C$	$C^{2\times3}$
Symmetry	$SO_3 + Wick$	$SU_2 \otimes SU_3$	$SU_2 \times gen.$
Q-Interpretation [2]	bit	probit	qubit
Classical forces	EM	Weak	Strong
Reinterpreted	Electro-Color Theory		

The three generations should appear as a Galois extension tower, so let us focus on the 1st generation.

The *only* external force is classical Electro-Magnetism, with its *Quantum Electro-Dynamics* (QED) quantum incarnation: the electron, as the data type carrying electric charge (external vertex /qubit) and the photon as the corresponding external quantum interaction channel (external edge -quantum channel-gate).

2. Triple Time

Since we aim to triple the time dimensions to achieve a total space-time symmetry, and since magnetism is related with the EM-current in the time like direction, we need to rewrite EM (later). The color charges seems to fit nicely as *three magnetic charges*, so we will attempt to unify EM and QCD, viewing the *colored quarks* from a generation as *magnetic charge qubits*. Confinement should be interpreted as follows: there are no free (whole) magnetic charges.

So magnetic charges are "time-like" and internal, while electric charges are "space-like" and external.

The IE-duality trading external DOFs ("space-time-matter") for internal DOFs (information-symmetry-entropy), should have a "carrier" accounting for the "missing energy": the neutrino! We thus try as an alternative to the

Fermi's model for the missing energy-momentum, to bestow on the neutrino the role of "internal-external mediator", between external electric charges (one) and internal magnetic charges.

The existence of fractional electric charges now corresponds to the existence of "fractional" magnetic charges, reflecting the space-time total symmetry via the generalized Wick rotation.

3. An Object-and-Relations Oriented Language

Besides the "external-internal" dichotomy we have the "object-symmetry" one imported from Category Theory, with entropy as a measure of symmetry, accounting for the "rest mass". This refines symmetry as due to external or internal DOFs.

It is natural to expect that gravity will emerge as an *organizational principle*, always attractive and minimizing external symmetry/entropy.

What about *anti-gravity*? A possible scenario to be orchestrated is that breaking internal symmetry increases entropy/mass, and by IE-duality, should compensate gravity

Gauge theory and fermion-boson dichotomy should still reflect the external leg - internal edge dichotomy, resolving the Fermi's 4-vertex effective theory.

Alternatively, other avenues are: symmetry of external space-time and gravity, symmetry of internal DOFs and QCD, as a dual *Electro-Color Theory*:

QDR	$E-Space$	$I-Space$	$E-Symmetry$	$I-Symmetry$
Ψ	Ψ_{space}	Ψ_{Spin}	$\Psi_{Isospin}$	Ψ_{color}
$\mathcal{O}$	(E,p)	Q_e	Q_q	(H,m).

4. Symmetry and Dark Matter/Energy

As explained in §1, energy-momentum corresponds to the "object level", while entropy-mass corresponds to the "symmetry level" of the object. They are combined at the level of the complexified action from the FPI: $\int e^{S/\hbar + iH}$.

Then symmetry is a candidate for the missing "dark matter/energy" needed to match observations in cosmology with the traditional models (classical mechanics, GR). We believe that accounting for symmetry in the context of a variable causal structure with duality is a flexible generalization for a new level of physics, with plenty of room for the "dark matter/energy". In any case, the fact that the current physics is not "almost done" since it seems that most of what's out there is ... missing (!), is a clear indication supporting our search for a new Equivalence Principle [23]. Recall that blowing-up time for a total unification of space and time via a generalized Wick rotation and doubling external space-time to include symmetry, must reflect on Einstein's mass-energy equivalence principle in a way compatible at the principial level with the current technical implementations (Higgs mechanism, black holes, dark energy etc.).

So far all the forces are modeled in the Standard Model (SM) using gauge theory. It is time to explore other more "divers" mechanisms (Non-Standard Models): not just R^4 and a gauge group G, but a mixture of space-time or more general causal structures, *and* symmetries!

CHAPTER 3

Q++: The Language of *Reality Design*

After replacing space-time with causal structures (e.g. Feynman graphs) and considering the QP-QC correspondence, the natural upgrade of gauge theory is *Quantum Information Dynamics* (QID) [**24**]: *quantum information flow* (quantum software) through *quantum circuits* (quantum hardware) [1].

Particle physics developed a language, the Standard Model (SM), which in fact describes quantum computing: physics prepares the Q-hardware (e.g. particle accelerators on one end of the scale and nanotechnology-quantum computers at the other) which will be capable of "producing" (running) the desired quantum computation.

A quantum interaction may be thought of a superposition of interaction modes, each pertaining to a common source and a common receiver as a target. It "collapses" under a measurement (quantum computation picture) to an external manifestation, the way the lightning strikes the ground (Feynman graph), except there is nothing else around the nodes and edges of the mode; it is a "vacuum" fluctuation but without an "ambient empty space".

---

[1]*Not* such a big step from RLC-circuits, as one might think!

1. Is There an "Elementary Reality"?

Probably not! The more we learn, the more we will refine our models including the elementary set of gates and its programming language $Q++$ [2].

Instead of searching the "Ultimate Theory", which must be unique and God given (that is the Number Theory), physics models will be like operating systems for the current generation of quantum hardware physicists will build, redesigning reality here and there as needed.

As a figure a speech for now, the Standard Model is the current "operating system" for the quantum hardware we build *to observe* "nature's elementary computations". It is perhaps time for some new and non-standard ideas *away from the tradition of the SM*, to start "running our own quantum computations", i.e. a dedicate quantum computing programming language $(Q++)$ and a new "operating system", as the title of the book suggests.

2. Why is Space 3D?

Probably because the internal basic symmetry of a qubit $SU(2)$ is "equivalent" (2:1) to the external symmetry $SO(3)$. Now $SU(2)$ has both the role of *quantum information* (QI) when interpreting a unitary matrix as a qubit, and it also has the role of *QI-processing*, when interpreted as a gate. Indeed, a qubit $q = z_0|0> + z_1|1>$ with $|z_0|^2 + |z_1|^2 = 1$ can be modeled as a unit quaternion, topologically S^3, or viewed in terms of Pauli matrices as an element of $SU(2)$ (gate). From the logic point of view, this amounts to view a qubit as a logic variable $z_0 Yes + z_1 No$ (the physicist's Up or Down spin), or as an elementary logical operation.

---

[2]Like the Goedel Theorems in mathematics, this gives hope there will always be excitement in science!

3. Quantizing Time

Time has the role of ordering events, classically shelved into synchronous layers ("foliating causality"). This is no longer the case when modeling quantum interactions using causal structures (Feynman categories).

Now, since energy and matter are quantized, and the causal network (discrete of finite type) is discrete too, what is time and is it quantized? We will refer to this *complexified* version of *Markov processes* as the (*Automaton Interpretation of QFT*).

Yes, "time" is quantized already! Since it lost its role of label per se, now all that remains are the labels "coloring" the nodes of the network: *the gates*; so the elementary "time click" is the unit of QI-processing, the quanta of quantum processing: the *qubit-gate SU(2)*!

Then it's a matter of measuring how many Q-gates (processing quanta) are there on a *computing path* from A to B. And various paths may take various "amounts of "processing time" (qubits). Now it is clear that processing-qubits are associated with sequential QC, i.e. "Time", while data-qubits are associated with parallel QC "Space". Since computing does not care about weather it's done one way or the other, the external super-symmetry/Wick rotation $(SU(2))$ is related to this duality.

In the correspondence between $SU(2)$ and $SO(3)$, we distinguish the "real rotations" and the "imaginary rotations". The *real rotations* of the complex basis of $\mathbf{C}^2$ as a real vector space are: $R(t) = (z_0 I + z_1 J)^2$ (Half-angle rational form: see 2D rotations done right using Clifford reflections). The *imaginary rotations* of the complex basis, the so called "internal symmetries", are

$$I^{\pm} = [e^{i\theta} \quad 0 | 0 \quad e^{\pm\theta}].$$

They can be interpreted as a *change of coefficients* $\mathbf{C}^2 = \mathbf{R}^2 \otimes_R \mathbf{C}$ and *lifting the symmetries*:

$$R(t) = R_t \otimes I, \quad I^+(\theta) = I \otimes R_\theta, I^-(\theta) = Conj \otimes R_\theta.$$

Choosing a prefered axis to establish the correspondence with R^3 should be viewed in the context of a triple time (3+3 total dimensions), i.e. considering two copies of $SU(2)$ (dynamical qubit [24]; see also bellow §6).

Returning to the quantization issue, the important measure of sequential computing is the length of the computation in terms of elementary gates ("time"), while the important measure for parallel computing is the memory capacity of the QI-channel ("space"). This should be related with the "odd fact" that QI of a black hole is proportional to its *area* (2-dimensional), not its volume.

So the volume form (distance-metric) should measure the quantity of information. If the causal structure admits a space-time coordinate system, then it should be a "product" of the *computational length* in qubits as units of processing quanta (time) and *memory capacity* again in terms of qubits as quanta of data (space) [3].

Additional "attributes" of the quantum communication channel should come from the external part (distance, momentum) in analogy with Kirchhoff's Laws for the scalar case (distance-resistance-conductivity [33]).

4. Logic, Statistics and Quantum Logic

The way we represent causality (causal structures, STCS) as a model for the "propagation of information" (1:1, n:1, 1:n) is reflected in the corresponding type of logic: *classical logic* ("Yes *xor* No" or $o, 1$), *probabilistic logic* ($0..1$) or *quantum logic* (qubits: "Yes and No"). To understand the measurement "paradox" we need to investigate the intermediary "reductions":

---

[3]Since there may be no STCS, the situation is more complicated; see Min-Cut-Max-Flow Theorem.

Logic:	Aristotelian	Probabilistic	Quantum
Coefficients:	$\mathbf{Z}_2$	$\mathbf{R}$	$\mathbf{C}$
Theory:	Counting Set Theory	Measure Spaces	Complex Geometry
Type:	L^1 - Discrete	L^1 - Real	L^2-Hilbert Spaces

To better compare the various theories, we need to distinguish the *change of coefficients* from the *change of type*, i.e. from counting (L^1) and set theory (analytical/constructive), to geometric (L^2) and category theory (algebraic/axiomatic).

Exponentiating classical logic yields the probabilistic logic:

$$P \in \mathbf{Z}_2^{R+}, ||P|| = 1 \quad P(1) = p, P(0) = 1 - p.$$

Complexifying probabilistic logic already delivers quantum logic:

$$Q \in \mathbf{Z}_2^{C}, ||Q|| = 1 \quad (qubit),$$

yet quantum mechanics is formulated as a geometry, requiring the benefic translation from a L^1-theory to an L^2-theory. This is achieved as a *square-root* (of course!) using spinors: Clifford algebras allow to take a square-root of a metric/measure to get a quadratic form:

$$d\mu \mapsto <, > \quad <=> \quad (|| \ ||_2)^2 = (|| \ ||_1)^2.$$

Clifford Algebras : *Quadratic Form* = (*Linear Form*)^2.

In the 1-dimensional case of classical logic, "tertium non datur" is always implied, so we think about logical values as *one value*: 0 xor 1, Y or No but not both, since the "complement" is uniquely determined:

Bit : $L = n|Yes > +m|No >, \ n, m \in \mathbf{N}, n + m = 1,$

Probit : $P = p|Yes > +q|No >, \ p, q \geq 0, p + q = 1.$

The big difference occurs when the value is 2-dimensional:

Qubit : $Q = a|Yes > +b|No >, \ a, b \in C, |a|^2 + |b|^2 = 1,$

i.e. "independent" or "dependent"? It depends!

Each of the two coefficients a and b have two additional orthogonal DOFs, allowing to implement a *correlation phase*. At $\theta = 0$ the two possibilities (Y and N) reinforce themselves, at $\theta = \pi/2$ they are "independent" (coexist), while at $\theta = \pi$ they interfere destructively; the new possibilities are ... amazing!

A natural mathematical implementation of the processing-qubit uses the ϕ^4-Riemann Surface (e.g. s/t electron-electron interaction etc.), or an equivalent decorated gadget.

5. *Motion* **Modeled as** *Teleportation*

Feynman diagrams are usually embedded in space-time and decorated with position, or dually with momenta after a Fourier transform. To get read of "ambient space" we need to account for "motion" in a different way: *teleportation!*

If internal states can be teleported, then in principle external states can be teleported also, as required by the IE-duality. What appears to be "continuous motion", and modeled by classical physics as such, can be modeled as *momentum teleportation* ("quantum network jumps") ... and therefore quantized, together with energy [4]. Although it might look like a drastic and "expensive" theoretical explanation, *quantum motion of a "particle"* can be modeled as a "wave" of network fluctuations ("vacuum fluctuations"), where the "vacuum" is NOT "empty *space*", but a state of network we are considering in the QDR formalism. We picture the motion of an electron as a sequence of pairs of creation followed by annihilation:

$$- (+-) \; (+-)...(+-) \quad - \; \mapsto \; -.$$

---

[4]This opens an avenue to investigate "alternative transportation" methods!

we emphasize that (we assume) there is *no space-time in the model apart from the causal modes of the Feynman Category being represented as a Feynman Process* [5].

6. Modeling the Particle-Antiparticle Pair

The pattern within logic, Y and N, spin up and down etc., as a "convex combination" with some specific coefficients suggests to investigate modeling not just an elementary particle alone, but together with its antiparticle.

Indeed, elementary particle physics will be modeled as *Quantum Information Dynamics* (QID) of *Feynman Processes* on *Feynman Categories* as *causal structures* [**24, 25, 26**] (see also [**29**]), by modeling how the *quantum bit of space-time-matter* modeled as a *data-qubit*, i.e. the unit/quanta of *quantum information*, *propagates* in a *quantum bit of time/causality*, modeled as a *qubit-gate*, i.e. a unit/quanta of *quantum information processing*. Therefore an elementary particle modeled as a qubit should be a super-position of the particle Ψ *and* antiparticle $\bar{\psi}$:

$$Q = \Psi|p> + \bar{\Psi}|\bar{p}> . \qquad (6.1)$$

Then, depending on the relative phase, this *dynamical qubit* (DQ) would model a particle in the Dirac's sea of particles with "negative energy", ready for a jump to a higher level (a photon producing a quantum phase change), becoming a pair of particle and antiparticle. A change of the relative phase towards destructive interference would model annihilation of the pair. Therefore, the creation/annihilation operators would be elementary qubit-gates.

A strong evidence for this approach is the mixtures of K_0-mesons, responsible for CP-violation [**10**]. This, in

---

[5]Therefore ... "Panta Rei"! The Greeks had a better intuition than we suspected.

turn can explain the presence of more matter than anti-matter, as a consequence of the existence of a time arrow, i.e. of a *direction of the quantum computation*. This is an "orientability" issue (e.g. orientation of manifolds), as an additional structure. Unitarity ensures reversibility, yet a quantum computation should include an "arrow of time" as the ordering of the data: from input to output.

Then QID could be implemented as a dynamics of the *Qubit Current* in the familiar Lagrangian formalism, but at the conceptual level, compiled into mathematics code based on a discrete model of finite type: *Quantum Network* (Feynman Category/Process, categorical language etc. - see [19]). Manifolds (continuum spaces) should NOT be used (see §2), since there is no "empty ambient space-time" apart from "energy-matter", not even a discrete one, as the discreetness of energy-matter is not compatible with a continuum model anyway. [6].

The knowledge accumulated in the Lagrangian formalism (from the *Standard Model*, say) can still be used, after a translation from the continuum framework to the discreet framework of the QDR. The interpretation in terms of quantum computing concepts is binded to it, "defining" the *Q++* quantum programming language to design the quantum software which will run on the quantum hardware built (*Quantum Reality Design*).

Returning to the mixture idea, another motivation for modeling pairs, or even triples, with respect to discrete symmetries is the mixture of generations of quarks [10].

The use of quaternions as qubits, implementing this "pairing" will facilitate the translation from the classical L^1-theory (probabilistic) to the L^2-theory (geometric) of quantum physics: Clifford algebras enable taking square-roots from quadratic forms, solving this problem

---

[6]And even if we solve the incompatibility issues, what if we need to simulate the model on a computer, classical or quantum!?

in a similar way complex numbers are needed for taking a square root of the symmetry flip of the real axis. This "time reversal" -1 is related to spin/fermion-boson statistics, since it equals two Wick rotations i^2 (see generalized Wick/time-to-space rotations §1, Equation 1.1).

7. Three Generations and Galois correspondence

The above mixtures, corresponding to discrete symmetries, is reminiscent of permutation actions and Galois theory/correspondence. The huge differences of mass between generations should correspond to a breaking of symmetry, similar to the reduction of the Galois group under the adjunction of a new root. This is due to a duality, which here probably is the IE-duality.

Now *colors* being thought of as magnetic charges (timelike QI-flow), the three generations could be the internal symmetry counter-part via such a duality.

8. Distance and Information Capacity

In classical physics *distance* is a primary concept (*metric space* etc.). in quantum physics the analogous primary concept is the Hermitean product (the "correlation angle"). A "merger" of these two views should involve a duality between the two. This is achieved by taking into account the CS-interpretation: distance as a measure of the capacity of interaction, which corresponds to quantum communication, should be dual to information capacity of a quantum communication channel. This is quite similar to the inverse of resistance in electric circuits ("RLC-Theory").

Specifically, since causality takes precedence to the space-like/time-like dichotomy, the capacity of *propagating quantum information* (qubits, data and gates) takes precedence to the classical idea of distance. In particular, one should change coefficients, moving away from a real to a complex "distance" [7]. We will explain latter how *mass* should be thought of *conjugate to distance*, in this complexified framework.

Complexification modeled as a change of coefficients, is an adjunction in the context of the IE-duality, so what is "the primary concept" is a "chicken-egg" situation.

9. Time and Causality

As almost always in the previous major advancements in physics, time is the key issue ... except in QM! So, it is time for a "makeover": time, as part of Space-Time Coordinate System (STCS), is a tentative *to order a quantum computation*; at a mathematical level, it amounts to factorize a Feynman Process (a representation of a Feynman graph/tangle etc.; see [**8, 7, 31**]).

So, time is not a fundamental concept; the Q-computation is the intrinsic concept, while space and time are just a "coordinate approach" (when there is one!).

The arrow of time is an orientation of a "reversible" Q-computation [8], when modeled by (i.e. relative to) a system capable of receiving and absorbing information (oriented: $I \to O$; we will revisit the CPT-issue latter on).

We think that "systems evolve in time", as an order / separation / foliation of events, and such that the "present" information cannot affect the "past". This is no longer "true" in a Feynman Process based on a category with duality, and, although *globally* there is an IO-orientation of the whole quantum computation of an interaction mode, locally the quantum information flow could be forward or backwards (anti-particles) when comparing the Feynman causal process (representation of a

---

[7]Conformal structure: correlation angles are needed!

[8]See Hermitean conjugation in a tensor category with duality [**30**].

diagram) with a particular factorization (STCS, operator product expansion OPE etc.).

In fact *loops* are the essential quantum corrections ("quantum feedback") which are the trademark of the (complex!) "Reality". The *Quantum-Info* → *Classical-Info* projection, due to the IE-adjunction (wave function collapse), cannot be order compatible (cannot order **C**!).

So, one has to develop the *Quantum Information Flow* as a of a Feynman Category generated by the elementary quantum logic gates [9]; to implement the *IE Duality* with its *Classical-Quantum Adjunction*, one needs to complexify the 2:1 $SU(2) → SO(3)$ correspondence:

$$Duality: \quad Ext/SO(3) \times Int/SU(2) \mapsto \mathbf{C}$$

Action Functor: Feynman Category → $SU_2 \otimes SU_3 - mod.$

The above prescription will become a blueprint when taking into account the present knowledge from *The Standard Model*.

The Classical-Quantum Adjunction will be explained as a *Logical Ladder*, from the $Z_2 → \mathbf{R} → \mathbf{Q}$ logic, with the mandatory reformulation from its combinatorial-probabilistic L^1-theory to its geometric L^2-theory formulation.

10. **What** *Space* **and** *Time* **Really Are**

As a "preview" of the mode technical discussion from [**31**], we present the main ideas developing the point of view that space-time is a coordinate system on a causal structure modeling a quantum computation-communication-interaction, with space-like separated events corresponding to parallel computing and time-like separated events corresponding to sequential computing. At the level of the represented process, the elementary particles will be represented as elementary gates processing the *only existing elementary particle*: the qubit (§4)!

----
[9]QID as a "non-abelian dynamics/time flow".

A quantum interaction is implemented as a morphism, and generically represented as:

$$I \overset{Gate}{\to} O.$$

The input elementary particles are "made" out of qubits, the gates are elementary interactions rephrased from the classical language of "force fields" and "distances" using the CS-language of *quantum gates, quantum information capacity* etc. (QFT as a "higher dimensional and noncommutative" RLC-Theory [**33**]).

At this point we note the "final" unification between the concepts of space and time into one, *causality as a quantum computation*, with the speed of light c playing the role of a conversion coefficient, with its dual conversion role between energy and mass/entropy.

In the new language, space-time-matter are already quantized, since quantum information is. The unit of time (Planck scale) is the "quantum click" (qlick: elementary gate processing, at a given frequency-momentum), as briefly mentioned earlier §3. The unit of space is, again, the qubit (quantum memory "location").

In a precise manner, introducing a STCS in the continuum limit relies on a space-time decomposition of a causal structure. This is essentially the *Min-Cut-Max-Flow Theorem*; it allows to represent a graph, say, as a bunch of dynamical paths, joining an initial "Cauchy surface" to a final Cauchy surface (see [**38**]).

The space-volume measures the number of disjoint paths (dynamic world lines), while the "time-length" of a path is the number of elementary quantum computations (qlicks) on a path. The *Mengel Theorem* relates the two pictures, i.e. cuts-Cauchy surfaces and Feynman paths-world lines, when replacing the number system from real numbers to quaternions. The usual positive flow in the above theorems becomes the qubit flow. The quantum capacity measures the density of information processing.

The tree interpretation of entropy allows to compute the entropy of the process. One has to generalize the theory to include non-trivial homology: the meshes determined by the edges not in the spanning trees are essentially the quantum corrections, i.e. vacuum fluctuations and non-zero Maxwell currents.

QID will be a reformulation of gauge theory in the FPI approach as a noncommutative Hodge-de Rham Theory of Feynman Processes [33].

A further discussion on what space and time really are, is postponed (see Ch. 5; [31]).

CHAPTER 4

Towards a Non-Standard Model (NSM)

We will present a few ideas regarding the import of knowledge from the Standard Model (SM) in the context of the Quantum Dot Resolution (QDR) with IE-duality.

As mentioned before, in the NSM there is only ONE generic "elementary particle", the qubit as *data*, i.e. an $SU(2)$-matrix represented as a quaternion:

$$SU_2(\mathbf{C}): \quad Q = z_1|Y> +z_2|N>.$$

There is only ONE "fundamental interaction", the qubit as a *gate*, i.e. an $SU_2(\mathbf{C})$ matrix with its Lie generator as a Hermitean form:

$$SU_2(\mathbf{C}): \quad U = e^{iX}, \quad X <=> v = (ct, x, y, z).$$

The entropy is a measure of (restricted) quantum symmetry:

$$SL_2(\mathbf{C}) = Aut(SU_2(\mathbf{C})) \Leftrightarrow Lorentz\ Transformations.$$

The determinant of the infinitesimal QI-current is the Minkowski "space-time" interval:

$$\text{``}Dual\ Bohr's\ Rule\text{''}: \quad det(X) = ||v||^2.$$

Now the crucial step away from SM and ST is "tripling time" [1].

---

[1][**24**]: "A fine print Evrika!"; perhaps a 3rd ST-revolution.

1. Quark Colors as Magnetic Charges

This prompts for rewriting electromagnetism (EM), and classical physics in general, since now "time" appears as a "polar radius" in the space of causal directions, and therefore, in the context of Noether Theorem, the *causal flow* is no longer scalar! We suggest that now, an appealing unification is that of EM and QCD (quantum chromodynamics); as suggested earlier, the quark colors are good candidates for internal magnetic charges, corresponding to the *vector charged current* in the causal direction ("magnetism"), and therefore "internal" and explaining the "asymmetry" in Maxwell's theory and the absence of "external" monopoles. This is consistent with a totally symmetric unification between space and time, therefore qualifying to an unification of EM and QCD in what we call the *Electro-Color Theory*:

$$EM + QCD \to QECD^2$$

$$SO_3 \times U_1 \ \& \ SU_3 \to SL_2(\mathbf{C}) \ acting \ on \ SU_2.$$

The 2×3 directions generate currents with corresponding charges:

$$Q_e = \pm 1, \quad Q_m = (R, G, B).$$

The quark flavors, i.e. the three generations, should be explained using a different mechanism §7, with an interface involving the concepts of mass, entropy and symmetry, compatible with the idea of breaking the symmetry and Higgs mechanism. There are plenty of opportunities regarding a well rounded theory without having to restrict modeling reality to the gauge fields and forces theme.

---

[2]Hodge-de Rham Theory on QDR [33].

In this spirit, we suggest to remap weak interaction phenomenology to the IE-duality, the implementation being postponed after the completion of $QECD$ [3].

2. Magnetic Charges and Confinement

The types of "internal matter" in the SM, i.e. mesons and barions, should be implemented as a consequence of the presence of three "time-like" dimensions (causality) in addition to the usual three space-like dimensions, and the corresponding projection relating the new description to the classical one:

$$"Effective\ Time": \quad 3D\ causality \rightarrow 1D\ time.$$

We will avoid technical arguments regarding the representation theory of SU_3 and argue at an intuitive level.

The presence of a time arrow/direction in the 3D-space of causal directions leads to a classification of the propagation of a qubit, similar to the spin and isospin classification of an electron ("external matter") and of a quark of a given color (and generation). The projections of a qubit correspond to the three colors ("internal charges"/magnetic charges). Accordingly this fragments the electric charge: $\pm 1/3, \pm 2/3$, yet the "particle" is the qubit, made out of three quarks.

To include a common explanation for barions and mesons, perhaps the particle-antiparticle "double picture" should be used §6. Then an elementary matter particle (barion) is a mixture:

$$Q = \Psi|p> + \Phi|\bar{p}>,$$

---

[3]And quantum gravity should be expected to emerge "for free", in a similar way it does in ST.

a combination similar to a quantum logic value, i.e. the qubit as a complex combination of Y and N (here of particle p and anti-particle p) [4]. The dynamical qubit (Equation 6.1) is made out of 3×2 quarks and anti-quarks, i.e. 3 "mesons" (quark-anti-quark pairs).

Recall that an "anti-particle" is a particle (quantum information) propagating backwards in time, as it is usually the case with representations of knots and tangles [7] (see also [8]). Therefore depending on the "angle" between the time-direction and qubit's causal direction, we should have first the dichotomy "particle-antiparticle" and second the 3 colors corresponding to a given coordinate system in the causal space. The *confinement* appears naturally, since the quarks are merely projections/components. The deep scattering experiments "proving" the existence of "externally separated" quarks definitely depends on the model used to interprete th experiments, model which is based on a continuum metric space-time $R^{3,1}$. Our suggestion amounts to "confine" the quark structure to internal space. "External space", e.g. Feynman diagrams, do not "live" in an external continuum space-time anyway; space distance and time distance are quantized.

3. Cooper Pairs and Color Current

A meson is a "Cooper Hermitean pair", for example $\pi = q_u \bar{q}_d$; there may be a relation with superconductivity (Cooper pairs of electrons with opposite spin $e_u e_d$), but since "internal matter" is complex, an additional conjugation (discrete symmetry) is required for the pair (gauge orbit). It is worth investigating if the QCD *internal magnetic current* can be modeled or related to the Cooper pairs mechanism for electric superconductivity.

---

[4]Or perhaps the "matter particle" is the real part and the anti-particle the imaginary part.

Now a "meson" does not live long, it is instable and disintegrates. The term "matter" refers to stable barions and their excited states, the *electron* (external; up-down spin) and *magneton* [5] (internal; up-down isospin, i.e. proton-neutron).

The "unstable matter" is modeled as "gates" and *quantum circuits* (mesons, resonances etc.). Recall that the qubit has a dual role. It has the role of data when it models the input and output data in a quantum computation, and it signifies "matter" from the application's point of view. It has the role of processing unit (gates and "algorithms", not necessarily elementary), when it processes quantum data/information [6].

The "weak interactions theory" is a reverse engineering of quantum algorithms in terms of elementary quantum gates.

The *data-gate* dichotomy naturally corresponding to particles and interactions, is a candidate for an alternative to the fermion-boson/particle-gauge field formalism, although it should admit a "simple" translation from the Hilbert space language to $Q + +$ (see [**9**]).

A dynamic qubit (Equation 6.1) could be the expression of supersymmetry; to break it, view the DQ as two fermions or three bosons.

On the other hand, the $SL_2(\mathbf{C})$ symmetry acts on qubit-data, as elementary operations/gates. What is the relation to the above speculations and entropy as a measure of symmetry remains to be seen. At this point let us recall that energy is conjugate to time, which is a "scalar" projection of causality. Entropy and information are the counterpart of energy and external matter,

---

[5]For symmetry reasons: electric/space-like, magnetic/causal.

[6]Building an elementary particle theory classifying elementary particles is the quantum computing analog of the theory of VLSI circuit design.

so a simple relation should be expected. It will be explained elsewhere that in the relativistic picture, mass is the conjugate quantity to the relativistic interval, both having a QC-interpretation in terms of qubits SU_2 and its symmetries $SL_2(\mathbf{C})$ [7].

Returning to the translation between gauge theory and data/gate formalism, a boson, say the photon for example, can be interpreted as a channel for a quantum interaction which is interpreted as a communication of quantum information. Recall that gauge theory represents a "resolution" of the 4-point Fermi interaction theory of "matter particles" into two 3-point interaction vertices where two IO-fermions interact via a *virtual boson* represented by an interaction line (current-current formalism). It is tempting to relate this resolution with the homology differential which inserts an edge at a vertex, the result being a superposition of all the possible IO-groupings.

So a meson or a resonance corresponds in the QDR formalism to the insertion of additional vertices by inserting another Feynman graph, and "resolving a phenomenological vertex" at a given resolution scale (degree).

The "life-time" of such an unstable particle should be derived from the time-length of a decomposition into elementary gates, measured in qlicks (see §3). At this stage we should appreciate the power of the homological approach using resolutions, where we are not constrained in a "fixed" and "ultimate" picture (elementary particle classification scheme), and where the only "elementary particle", the qubit (data/gate) is the building material of the quantum software corresponding to the quantum hardware: *quantum circuits created by experimental physicists* [8] in particle accelerators in various

---

[7]Distance/conductivity in the internal space of symmetries.

[8]The analog of lightning, as an essentially electric discharge.

forms depending on the designed hardware (energy available, various sources, filters and receptors of quantum information etc.).

4. Three Generations and Entropy

Entropy as a measure of symmetry plays a fundamental role: it is a generator of mass, a quantity conjugate to the relativistic "space-time" interval.

The projection of causality onto a radial time-direction leads to mixtures of quarks in reinterpretation of the fundamental representation of SL_2 on $su(2)$, which corresponds to adjoint action by conjugation on qubits $SU(2)$.

A representation theoretic argument should lead to the three generations of quarks, with appropriately different symmetry groups (breaking of symmetry and Galois correspondence §7), and therefore to different masses.

The "coefficient category" to be used to represent a *Feynman Category* as a *Feynman Process* (*Feynman Current Algebra*) should be a braided category with duality [**7**] affording the SL_2 and SU_3 actions ($SL_2 - mod - SU_3$ Clifford algebras):

$$\mathbf{C} \to V^* \otimes V, \quad V \otimes V^* \to \mathbf{C}.$$

This should reflect the factorization of a dynamical qubit into a pair of barion-antibarion or three mesons (pairs of quark-antiquark):

$$Q_B \oplus \bar{Q}_B = DQ = \oplus_{\sigma \in S_3} \ \sigma(Q_M).$$

One may ponder on the possible role of skein relations in connection to the above "quantum skein relation" between barions and mesons, for example within the 1st generation $Q_B = uud$ and $Q_M = u\bar{d}$ (unit, counit, $T(V \oplus V^*)$).

CHAPTER 5

Hopf objects: Doubling Everything!

The operation of doubling [1] is essential to quantization (e.g. bialgebra quantization, quantum double, renormalization as a factorization [2] deformation quantization and renormalization [20] etc.).

The role of quantization as a deformation can be understood from the homotopical perturbation theory (HPT) perspective (deformation theory) [27]. We claim that the Heisenberg uncertainty relations represent the signature of a homological resolution (contracting homotopy). For example the fermionic CCR satisfied by the annihilation-creation operators correspond to the homological and cohomological differential inserting and collapsing DOFs in the QDR:

$$\{a, a^*\} = 1 \quad \leftrightarrow \quad [d, d^*] = Id.$$

What remains to be understood is the "external-internal" adjunction between the "real DOFs" (classical space-time-matter and logic) and "complex DOFs" (quantum information and logic; data and processing).

We will inspect the relations between $SU(2)$, SO_3 and $SU(3)$, to better understand the correspondence between "classical" $SO_3(\mathbf{R})$ and "quantum" $SU_2(\mathbf{C})$.

Recall that the "format" (or lack of one) of the present text is that of a research journal. The facts and interpretations will be distilled later on [33].

---

[1] ... a *categorification* in a set-theoretical disguise!

[2] Again corresponding to the underlying categorification to construct a Hopf object [17].

1. Energy and Mass

The role of speed light c is one of conversion between energy and mass $E = mc^2$, which in a classical model for space-time appears primarily as a conversion between space and time $s = ct$ ("real Wick rotation").

Assuming that "space" (parallel processing) and "time" (sequential processing) are orthogonal relative to a STCS, we think of space and time as a quadratic extension [3] (towards a Wick rotation interpretation):

$$E = km, \quad Event = s + \sqrt{k}t \quad (c = \sqrt{k}).$$

To prepare a connection with quantization, we recall the wave-particle duality in the form of elementary relations between the basic corresponding concepts (Plank, de Broglie etc.):

$$Particle: \ E^2 - kp^2 = (m_0 k)^2,$$

$$Wave: \ E = h\nu, \quad p = c^{-1}k.$$

Quantization will result from a reduction to (analysis of) information "gain and loss" ("created and destroyed"; recall that *quantum information is conserved*: it cannot be duplicated/copied!): "integer flux" [4] (current-symmetry-action formalism relative to the discrete measure, and translated in geometric language). The classical information theory (Shannon-Wiener entropy) assumes that information is only gained or only lost. For decision trees, information current and information gain see [24]) while quantum information theory has to deal with Feynman graphs possibly including loops/circuits (creation and destruction; multiplication and comultiplication; bialgebras and PROPs [26]).

---

[3]The *field of fractions* s/t can be thought of as a linear extension towards algebraic completion, for which rotation is the inversion - see bifields, antipode, Hopf objects etc.

[4]Is there a "charge" for a coproduct?

The need of implementing creation of DOFs is reflected in the need for introducing graphs (beyond trees and partitions) for which a node may have several inputs (parents) besides having several outputs (descendents).

Graphs are related to the operation of "gluing" a tree and a cotree, and the reverse operation: factorizing a graph into a tree and a cotree. This in turn is related to the introduction of a STCS.

This process of representing a graph $\Gamma = ts^{-1}$ as a "fraction" of trees, can be thought of as a linear extension in the same way a field of fractions is like a linear extension: doubling and factoring by a relation.

At the level of metric spaces (inner product spaces) such a representation needs square-roots: Clifford algebras (see [15]).

For operators which have dual symbols via Fourier transform or some other duality, this corresponds to introducing a Dirac operator as a square-root of the Laplacian. The general homological algebra setup of factorization (Hodge-de Rham Theory; see also [33]) and the need for quantization as a deformation of structure is sketched in [27] (see also [26]).

2. Wick Rotations

The point is that probabilities correspond to collapsing (tree hierarchy/ multiplication etc.) while conservation of matter-information in the context of duality (creation/ destruction; categories with duality; destructive/ constructive interference etc.) needs an additional degree of freedom beyond the "linear theory" (real line $\mathcal{R}$ etc.). It needs a rotational degree of freedom in the direction of propagation of information ($\mathbf{C}$, $SU(2)$ decorations of graphs, Riemann surfaces etc.). The "minimal model" is the qubit, the unit of quantum logic:

$$Q = z_1|Y> +z_2|N>.$$

The "merger" and "unfolding" of "possibilities" while still satisfying a conservation law, can be achieved via a rotation in the "merger" direction and "unfolding direction":

Representing Wick rotation:

$$z_1 \times multiplication \oplus z_2 \times coproduct.$$

This "algebraic Wick rotation" leads to bialgebras etc., in contrast with the original Wick rotation ict ("tangent space Wick rotation") which leads to the analytical representation of PROPs with Wick rotation: Riemann surfaces and CFT.

The universal Boolean bialgebra (without the lattice axiom - see [24]) is probably the "Boolean algebra" of quantum logic (in analogy with trees/partitions/power sets and Boolean logic). Recall that any Boolean algebra is a subalgebra of a power set Boolean algebra. The connection with gates and hardware is made via the "theory of circuits": representations of graphs.

So the need for complex numbers is now clear: conservation of information (numbers) in the context of a resolution with duality (creation and annihilation satisfying Heisenberg's uncertainty relation; Hodge-de Rham Theory).

This prompts again for tripling the time, towards a total time-space Wick super-symmetry. The alternative is a Kahler structure $I^2 = J^2 = K^2 = -1$, representing the three possible Wick rotations, or another way said, quaternions ($SU_2(C)$ or Clifford algebra) [5].

3. 2nd Order or 1st Order Differential Equations?

The need for Clifford numbers is rooted in the relation between the infinitesimal description (tangent space) and the need for a double. One can "square" the linear

---

[5]Fortunately $2 \times 3 = dimT^*(S^3) = 3 + 3 \times 1$.

case, leading to 2nd order differential equations (principal symbols), or double the description ($TM \oplus T^*M$, Manin triples, Drinfeld double, etc.) and deform (gluing) towards a Hodge duality.

The second algebraic picture is by far more symmetrical and convenient, so the need to pass from the classic Newtonian picture (2nd ODE) to the algebraic double picture (1st order on the double space: Lie algebra-UEA etc.) leads to Dirac operators and spinors, via quantization (see bellow §6).

A 2nd ODE/PDE (Laplacian picture) can be translated into a 1st ODE either via dynamic systems (one 2nd ODE = system of 2 1st ODEs) or (better) rephrased as an integro-differential equation (e.g. Boltzmann's equation).

An example which is prototypical in the context of Hodge-de Rham theory [33] is provided by the Maxwell methods / Kirchoff's Laws for electric RLC-circuits. Instead of a 2nd ODE focusing on charge:

$$L\frac{d^2Q}{dt^2} + R\frac{dQ}{dt} + \frac{1}{C}Q = E,$$

one can "double the space" $I = dQ/dt$ the current and V the potential ("cocurrent") and model the circuit by a Hodge duality $V = ZI$, e.g. $V = RI$. Then, in a differential model (no derivatives/slopes!), the Kirchoff's laws are linear:

$$Conservation\ of\ Charges \quad dI = 0$$

$$Current\ Sources = d^*I.$$

Incidentaly, there is no need to symmetrize the two laws by introducing "magnetic charges"; the symmetry is here a duality, and the description in terms of current I is symmetrical to the description in terms of cocurrent V, the potential (see Maxwell's methods).

On the other hand $\int$ plays the role of a contraction in a Hodge-de Rham 1-CW complex (etc. - see [27, 33]).

To implement the above Hodge duality picture needs a doubling process which will be discussed in §7. The resulting framework is that of the Dirac operator, as a square-root of the Laplacian.

In the Clifford bundle with a connection formalism ("tangent bundle picture"), the Dirac operator is [40]

$$\partial = \partial \cup A + \partial \wedge A.$$

In the cotangent picture", in terms of differential forms:

$$\partial = d - \delta, \quad \partial \wedge = d, \ \partial \cup = \delta,$$

where d and δ are the Hodge-de Rham differential and codifferential. ∂ is also called the Dirac-Kahler operator.

In [27, 3] it was noted that the more general framework ("the interface") is that of a *partial contraction* (a "contraction" but without the trivial homology assumption) which in homotopy perturbation theory is also called *strong deformation retract* [2]. Then the Dirac operator is a deformation of one of its "halves", and *Maurer-Cartan equation* is the Laplace equation (*Master Equation*):

$$\partial^2 = 0 \Leftrightarrow \Delta = 0,$$

i.e. the *harmonic forms* are the "flat connections" in Chen's sense (no "matter/sources" present), or *deformations* (quantizations) of the "classical picture" ("half" of the "bi-structure"). The *moduli space* of the space of deformations is the quotient relative to the *gauge equivalence*. Quantization relies on the Hodge *-operator as a duality, i.e. compatibility between the two structures of the bi-structure (e.g. bialgebra deformation quantization with r-matrix etc.); the more general picture is again that of a partial contraction [27].

The presence of "mater" is detected as curvature of the connection, in the same spirit with GR.

Now, if we "loose the base space-time" and consider the algebraic picture instead, we can develop the *Hodge-de Rham-Dirac-Kahler Theory on Feynman Processes* (in particular on the *Quantum Dot Resolution*): representations of quivers and their associated path categories can be thought of as bundles over 1-CW-complexes, and "import" gauge theory in the discrete framework [**33**] (more details later: §6), with **the same interface**.

Here we only note that the *Maxwell equations*, which are the continuum tensor analog of *Kirchoff's Laws of Electric Circuits*, are in differential form two (4 in vector formalism):

$$Maxwell's\ Equations:\quad dF = 0,\ \delta F = J.$$

In the "double formalism" of Dirac's operator obtained by taking a Clifford square-root we obtain:

$$Maxwell - Dirac\ (Linear)\ Equation:\quad \partial F + J = 0.$$

To symmetries the Maxwell Equations magnetic charges, monopoles, were introduced; in the present context this leads to

$$\partial F + \mathcal{J} = 0,\quad \mathcal{J} = J + *K,$$

where K is thought of as the magnetic current (!?) and $*K = Ke_5$ [**40**].

Why symmetrize Maxwell's equations or Kirchoff's laws!? The 1st equation is the conservation of the current, while the 2nd equation represents the boundary conditions (sources are attached to the geometric / categorical boundary).

We believe that the "correct" symmetrization between electricity and magnetism should be done at the level of the duality *external-internal*. In our NSM the color of quarks (internal qubits) are the magnetic charges ($SU(3)$ symmetry: three causal directions), while electric charges ("colors" of external qubits: leptons, without neutrino which is an energy-momentum conservation "issue") are the real manifestation of particle-antiparticle symmetry ("time reversal").

$$\begin{array}{lccc}
 & Kirschoff'sLaws & & Hodge-deRham \\
External & dI = 0 \quad V = \delta\phi & & dF = 0 \quad \delta F + J = 0 \\
Duality & V = *I & & J = *K \\
Internal & \cdots & & d\bar{F} = 0 \quad \delta\bar{F} - K = 0.
\end{array}$$

The relation between the "symmetrization" on the double with Hodge duality, and the *Min-Cut-Max-Flow Theorem* will be explained elsewhere [**32**, **33**].

4. Probabilities and Amplitudes (revisited)

The main need for "doubling", beyond the formal aspect or convenience (1st or 2nd order), is the need to model creation and collapsing of DOFs not just "loss of information"; *multiplication* or *grouping*, i.e. power sets, leads to decision trees (partitions and trees/forests), or better still, to "preimage calculus" (simplicial objects):

$$X \xrightarrow{f_1} X \xrightarrow{f_2} \dots \xrightarrow{f} X.$$

This suggests "non-deterministic dynamics" (statistics): DOFs (or information regarding them) may be "hidden" in a given stage of the description, and through information gain new internal structure may "appear". The deterministic dynamics analysis (evolution forward in time) has to be supplemented by "tracing back in time" $f^{-1}(Y)$, $Y \subset X$ (the above "preimage calculus").

In the quantum picture, which cannot be linearized by ordering the correlations in a $time \times configuration-space$ $event$-$space$ (§6), DOFs "appear" and "dissappear" as vacuum fluctuations; these are modeled as insertion and collapsing DOFs in the QDR ("zoom in/out": d and d^*). This requires a doubling of each bit: the qubit as a "gluing" of two bits (see bellow).

Probabilities are related to *amplitudes* (of probability) according to the *Bohr's Rule*:

$$P = |A|^2.$$

The comparison between the classic and quantum theory is more difficult because of the different languages used: L^1-measure theory (real probability) versus L^2-measure theory (Hilbert spaces - complex geometry).

Probability theory can be "geometrized" first by replacing the convex combination correlation,:

$$Probability: \quad p|Y > +q|N >, \ p + q = 1,$$

with its trigonometric form, we will call a *probit*:

$$Geometric\ Phase\ Correlation: \theta, \quad p = \cos^2\theta, \ q = \sin^2\theta.$$

Of course the $\pm$ ambiguity can be traced back to the projective space of lines (infinitesimal geodesics / world lines, momenta etc.) §6.

Then we get a 2:1 (!) covering map:

$$Probit: \ L^2(S^1) \to L^1[0, 1], \tag{4.1}$$

$$Q_R(\theta) = \cos\theta|Y > +\sin\theta|N > \mapsto P = \cos^2\theta.$$

This is the *real version of Bohr's rule.* Lifting probability theory to a "real" (better still: rational) geometric theory can be done by "taking a square-root" (real Clifford algebras).

This leaves to explain "complexification", i.e. the need to change coefficients from R to C (doubling the dimension).

It will be argued bellow that the use of real numbers is due to the "wrong" mathematical approach to "complete" the integers: constructing fields of fractions instead of Hopf objects (*bifields*, Riemann sphere $\mathbf{C}P^1$ etc.) §6. At this stage it is enough to point to the fact that probabilities *are* fractions *favorable events/all events*, while the symmetric picture is a linear equation $k\ Yes + l\ No = n\ All$. This amounts from the "physics" point of view to study the flow of event possibilities, i.e. *counting amounts* ([**24**], information flux and charge etc.), instead of "reducing to percentages", i.e. considering the corresponding projective geometry (see the *Boltzmann Correspondence* [**24**], the energy and the entropy pictures and the interpretation of the partition function as an L^1-norm).

Schematically:

Mathematics		*Physics*
Q Rationals	Measure	Wigner
R Reals	Theory	Measure
↑ *Field of Fractions*		
Z	Q : *Analysis or Geometry?* A : *Algebra!*	
↓ *Hopf Rings*		
$\mathbf{C}P^1$ Riemann	Hilbert	CFT
Sphere	Spaces	TQFT

More details will be given bellow §5, including how to *avoid* real numbers, and still get the complex *rational* numbers.

5. "Forget" *Fields!*

The evolution of number systems is marked by completions, addressing the need to solve equations:

$$N \subset \mathbf{Z} \subset \mathbf{Q} \subset\subset \mathbf{R} \subset \mathbf{C} \subset \mathbf{H} \subset \mathbf{O} \ etc..$$

The procedure always involves a doubling, *except* the analytical completion to get the reals (beware of limits!). Briefly said, the integers should be viewed as a Hopf ring.

DEFINITION 5.1. The Hopf ring $(\mathbf{Z}, \cdot, \Delta)$, with the coproduct

$$(p, q) \mapsto n = p \cdot q, \quad \Delta n = \sum_{p \cdot q = n} p \otimes q,$$

is called the *universal Hopf ring*.

The combinatorial aspects entailed by the coproduct would lead to a *Number Theory as the shadow of Quantum Field Theory* (for an article supporting the well-known general feeling, see D. Kreimer - "Numbers we should now").

Then one can "do" geometry (Lie theory): Lie algebra of *primitive elements*, the prime numbers, universal enveloping algebras (UEA) and dynamic systems etc. Bialgebras and quantization is the natural generalization as a *higher dimensional Lie theory* [**27**]: *Deformation Theory*, Maurer-Cartan equation and algebraic-formal connections (Chen), gauge theory and Yang-Mills theory etc.

In conclusion, "forget real numbers"; all we need is a Hopf structure, e.g. mutiplication and divisibility.

At the categorical level, all we need is a *braided category* with duality for a Hilbert space formalism of finite type (the completion of a pre-Hilbert space is not needed; the "continuum limit" should be avoided, as it collapses the quantum structure!), e.g. type II_1-subfactors and topological quantum field theory (TQFT) - see [**30**].

To evaluate the "Hopf object" alternative, we need to reexamine why do we need fields in the first place; and in the commutative world they may be "OK", but in the non-commutative world the complications due to having left and right fractions (ORE rings etc.) already suggest there is trouble afoot!

Mathematically, "fractions" are needed when comparing two quantities (size/mass) representing two objects, leading to the concepts like *distance* etc.

The two objects should rather be thought of as in 2-dimensions (in the Q-world there are no 2-alike fermions or quantum states: No Cloning Theorem!). Then the "relation" (comparison) is better represented by a "line" (vector: correlation/Q-event):

$$r = kX - lY \quad (ordered \ pair : (k,l) \cong arrow : k \to l),$$

showing the need and presence of *categorification*.

On the other hand, in a "Digital World", all should be quantized and measured in quanta, so natural numbers/counting and orientation/integers should suffice.

The field of fractions may be thought of as "linear extentions", for example the rationals:

$$\mathbf{Q} <=> \mathbf{Z}[\mathbf{Z} \times \mathbf{Z}]/ < n(m,n) - m > .$$

6. What is *Speed*, Really?

From the physics perspective, the field of fractions is required to define speed, in our attempt to order correlations based on labeling events using a (relative) distance, in a space-time (STCS) **with-out a maximal speed** (slope l). Then each rational speed s/t is a "causality cone": all lines of all slopes representing equivalent fractions, i.e. "passing" through the same x-intercept:

Rational Numbers   <=>   Causal Cones.

Now the existence of a maximal speed is a hint of a **discrete projective theory**: [6]

Special Relativity + QM $\Rightarrow$ Quantum Field Theory.

Speed as slope is an attempt to "linearize" a 2-dimensional causal structure, i.e. foliate the "geodesics" (the Feynman Category of paths), i.e. to introduce a STCS. In a similar manner as for "fields", we need to double it back: *Hopf Objects.*

---

[6]"Einstein + Planck·Heisenberg => Dirac".

Again from the physics perspective, to "eliminate speed", we need to compare two "motions/evolutions". In fact this reduces to comparing the two possible paths of a double slit experiment ("the mother" of all quantum behavior - R. Feynman): its representation is **the qubit!** §9 Briefly said, paths have local times (phases) and distances traveled are a consequence of differences in path lengths, information encoded by the qubit together with the associated probability (Feynman Categories are 2-categories enriched over $SU(2)$/quaternions /qubits). Now imposing a STCS on such a representation of the qubit flow in a causal structure should yield both special relativity and spin statistics, i.e. QFT.

7. Hopf Objects

A special case of a Hopf object is the Riemann sphere. This was previously called by the author "bifields" ([**24**]), yet its need was much older than this; one would like to make sense of the duality between 0 and ∞ etc.

So fields are needed to **order causality** in the cartesian product of pairs of events st^{-1}, yet they loose the "time dimension", becoming a commutative mathematical structure: $st^{-1} = t^{-1}s$. From the physics perspective (distance interpretation) a particle reflected in the future as an antiparticle is the same the antiparticle reflected in the past. In the same way QFT needs relativistic formulation (to allow creation / annihilation), we claim that the speed of light c as a maximum speed is correlated to the existence of a quanta of action $energy \times time$ in a integer formulation of QFT (Hopf objects) as an information flow (qubit dynamics).

Restoring the "Hopf Object" picture requires, of course "doubling back" the completion:

$$0 \to \mathbf{Z} \to \mathbf{Z} \times \mathbf{Z}^* \to \mathbf{Q} \to 0.$$

If we trace back the construction one more step, we see the relevance of the diagonal in doubling back $\mathbf{Z}$ towards the original picture: $m \to n$ (shadow of category theory on sets etc.).

Now the natural course of action is to *avoid division* [7] (as well as forgetting limits, i.e. the continuum) and consider the antipode (inversion) instead, to avoid entering in a "chiral world" (left or right?). The field of complex numbers should be replaced by the "bifield" $(\mathbf{C}_{North}, +, \cdot), (\mathbf{C}_{South}, \oplus, \cdot), S : \mathbf{C}_N \to \mathbf{C}_S$, where:

$$S(z) = 1/z, \quad z_1 \oplus z_2 = z <=> S(z) = S(z_1) + S(z_2),$$

consisting from the two stereographic projection chart atlas of the Riemann sphere $\mathbf{C}P^1$ (two copies of $\mathbf{C}$ isomorphic via the antipode S). One should immediately recognise the "series addition" $z = z_1 + z_2$ and the "parallel addition" $1/z = 1/z_1 + 1/z_2$, corresponding to the rule of computing the resitance in electric circuits for example.

But this is the **space of qubits** in disguise $B_N \oplus B_S$, consisting of the unit quaternions $(SU(2))$ with positive real part and respectively negative real part, unit disks glued on the unit 2d-sphere of pure quaternions.

The geodesics on the Riemann sphere (pairs of events away from the diagonal: affine projective space) are a "double of the Riemann sphere" corresponding to the quaternions.

In conclusion: "no slopes / derivatives", better lines/ differential forms (infinitesimal level), which of course it is well known! This motivates yet again replacing the Newtonian picture of a space and time coordinate system with the Feynman's picture of path/ histories causality structure. In this framework a "speed limit" relative to a

---

[7]Grothendieck $\sim$ remember the groupoid, not just the moduli space.

STCS c should exist as a direct consequence of quantizing interactions $\hbar$; there is no apriori difference between what macroscopically we call space and time, and c plays the role of a conversion factor in our biassed description of "change". Additional "clues" should be found in Penrose's Twistor Theory.

From the mathematical point of view, "fields" are the natural path towards algebraic completion in the *commutative world*; otherwise the completion with a promising future in the non-commutative world is the Hopf object (bifield).

8. ... and String Theory?

String Theory struggled to find the right number of space-time dimensions to embed Riemann surfaces, only to struggle even harder to get rid of most of them via compactification. By now there are physicists who "feel" that this number is irrelevant. And indeed infinitely many would do (Brownian motion etc.).

But STCS may not necessarily exist, and when they do, one would have to struggle quantizing them (Quantum Gravity etc.).

The easy way out is to keep the really revolutionary idea underlying String Theory: the "2-dimensional time" ($SU(2)$/qubits) appearing in the disguise of Riemann surfaces with its natural Wick rotation manifesting itself as st-duality (CFT - see [24]).

The *string*, open or closed, should not be thought of as acquiring an additional external dimension; it is parameterized anyways as one space-like dimension and one time-like dimension (see [13]). The string (just an amplitude z_i), or rather a bunch of "interacting strings" and represented as a pointed Riemann surface (RS; holomorphic disks removed) models a quantum gate processing a bunch of qubits. Since two holomorphic disks form a qubit, it is expected that one needs to include the anti-holomorphic sector too.

In conclusion, there is no need to embed RS in a Newton-Einstein space-time, but study the Segal PROP directly, as one studies group theory in abstract, usually after the representation theory is well developed for historical reasons.

The additional structure on a Feynman Category needed instead of a representation seems to be a homotopy structure (2-category structure) representing the information data: paths correlated by qubit-data. The "collapse of the wave function" appears as an *averaging process* prototypical of the *stable phase approximation* which allows to obtain the classical Lagrangian picture as a continuum classical limit.

9. Qubit Flow and Motion

The parallel-sequential duality, in addition of the above Hodge duality, means that space and time are dual (see Wick rotation).

Information (qubits) travels with the speed of light c (phase speed), which is a universal conversion factor between space and time, and energy and mass.

Now the "classical motion" is a "Brownian teleportation walk" with the relativistic speed as an effective (group) speed.

To better understand the relation between space, time and speed (see also §6), we need to "double" again, not to assume a "universal time/space" structure, not even locally (no classical determinism etc.).

Comparing to "motions", i.e. quantum events with the same source and target can be modeled as a homotopy structure, or equivalently a 2-category, more precisely defining the 2-morphisms as qubits.

DEFINITION 9.1. A *Feynman Process* is a 2-category for which $Hom_1(S,T)$ are dg-coalgebras and the 2-morphisms are qubits $Hom_2(\Gamma_L, \Gamma_R) = SU_2(\mathbf{C})$.

More details on the classical correspondence (quantum and classical sources and targets, classical and quantum gates etc.) will be given later on §9.

The qubit captures both particle and wave properties, i.e. the *particle-wave duality* as well as *Bohr's Rule* are consequences of the above framework. A qubit represents a correlation between quantum-events. As stated by Feynman in a suggestive way, the double slit experiment is the "mother of all quantum experiments". The two slits "split" the classical particle (source) into a qubit: it is a *quantum source* (path splitter/external creation of possibilities: it is the universal dichotomy in the quantum logic).

10. Hopf Rings and Fields: Amplitudes and probabilities

Hopf rings encode both creation and destruction of possibilities, leading to the quantum picture, while the usual ring - field construction leads to probabilities.

In $H = (\mathbf{Z}, \cdot, \Delta)$ with g the primitive elements (primes) the projective infinitesimal picture $\log k / \log n + \log l / \log n = 1$ leads to decision trees, factorization and quantization. Line bundles over $\mathbf{C}P^1$/ Riemann surfaces reflect the basic S^1-Hopf fibration of qubits/amplitudes and probabilities. Recall that qubits $SU(2)$ ($|z_1|^2 + |z_2|^2 = 1$: topologically S^3) form an S^1-fibration over S^2 (Riemann sphere/bifield).

CHAPTER 6

Feynman Categories and Quantum Sources and Gates

A *Feynman Category* is alternatively defined as a 2-category, where the 2-morphisms are interpreted as transformations of qubits, i.e. Lorentz transformations [1]:

$$Source \xrightarrow[\substack{Qubit\_path2}]{\overset{Qubit\_path1}{\Downarrow Lorentz}} Target.$$

Recall that qubits are $SU_2(C)$ matrices and their infinitesimal generators are Hermitean forms corresponding to Minkowski events, while the transformations are $SL_2(C)$ matrices corresponding to proper Lorentz transformations: changing "space-time coordinates" from one moving-frame on one path (the "from" path) to another moving-frame on the other path ("to" path).

As Feynman put it, the double slit experiment is the mother off all quantum experiments; in a mathematical translation, the 2-morphism is the essential additional structure element to the category of paths representing the possible transitions of the quantum system being modeled.

---

[1] Regarding the notation, we prefer to encode more meaning in the notation by using longer identifiers then just the customary "letters" from mathematics; alphabets have limitations, and such a short notation is too much dependent on the author. We aim towards a global interface; letters will be used as volatile objects, at the level of the author-dependent implementation, which should be well isolated from the user-interface.

1. *Bohr's Rule* is a Corollary

A 2-morphism is also a *quantum gate* (QG), since it processes a qubit and outputs in general another qubit.

DEFINITION 1.1. Such a 2-morphism is called a *quantum-path-splitter*. If it is the identity 2-morphism, then we call it a *quantum-phase-splitter*, which generates one qubit. Both are referred to as *quantum sources* (QS).

If the relative amplitude of a uni-path quantum source is zero:

$$Q = e^{i\theta}(cos(t)|Y > +sin(t)|N >) \quad (\theta_1 = \theta_2 = \theta),$$

then it is called a *classical source* of probability $\cos^2 t$, with associated *probit*:

$$P = \cos t|Y > +\sin t|N > .$$

That the *amplitude of probability of a classical source* is the projection on the first component, called the *real part* of its probit:

$$A = Re(P) = \cos t \ e^{i\theta}.$$

From definitions we obtain the following

LEMMA 1.1. **Bohr's Rule**: $P = |A|^2.$

2. Meet the Parents of Quantum Physics

In a way the "mother and father" of quantum phenomena is the quantum erasure, say realized as a double measurement of a quantum source, for example as in [16]; we prefer to simplify the picture and consider electrons in a double slit experiment "viewed" using an electron-microscope, instead of using light for the detection of which-way information.

Besides the two quantum sources, the two qubits generated by the quantum-path-splitter-gate (PSG) and the "auxiliary" probing qubit, we have two *classical sinks*

/ *targets* (CT) represented by the two *classical measure-ments*: registration of "one" electron on the photographic plate (or whatever *classical event counter*/number of particles) and the registration of the "other" electron by the electron microscope:

$$\begin{array}{ccc} \textit{Double Slit} & \textit{with} & \textit{Quantum} \\ \textit{Experiment} & & \textit{Erasure} \end{array}$$

$$(QS)$$

$$QS \xrightarrow{Qubit_1} PSG \underset{Qubit\_path2}{\overset{Qubit\_path1}{\rightrightarrows}} Q - Chip \xrightarrow{Out\_Signal_1} CS_1$$

with $Qubit_2$ arrow down into $Q-Chip$ and Out_Signal_2 arrow down to

$$CS_2.$$

It is clear by now that the "counting process" mandated by the classical measurements conforming to classical boolean logic will clash with the "quantum counting", where the *number of qubits* is not conserved (creation and annihilation of "particles"), yet the *quantum information current* **is conserved** (QI can't be copied unless it is destroyed: No Clone Theorem etc.).

As an additional simplification, replace the plane surface where the interference occurs with another "classical detection" devise: the classical sink #2.

The detailed analysis of the quantum erasure "family" will appear elsewhere.

3. 2-Morphisms and Quantum Gravity

As a "rabbit out of the magic quantum hat" comes quantum gravity.

The above coincidence of notation for a quantum gate (QG) is not accidental: small "acceleration increments" in Einstein's free falling elevator which compensates gravity can be modeled as "small" changes of inertial frames, therefore being quantum gates, mathematically implemented as 2-morphisms and allowing to formalize quantum gravity!

$$Free\ Fall \cong Quantum\ Amplitude\ Transfer.$$

The "ultimate quantization" occurs when we will finally quantize the last continuum quantity standing: the quantum phase. Then the "algebraic picture" (Feynman Processes) and the "geometric picture" (Klein-Galois Theory) will unveil the "ultimate picture of particle physics": number theory (Theory of Hopf Objects).

4. The S^1-Hopf Fibration

The relation between probability theory (classical logic) and quantum theory (quantum logic) can be better understood in connection with the Hopf fibration (Clifford algebras) $S^3 \to S^2$ (see [**15**]).

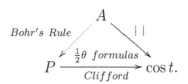

This allows to better understand the role of quantum-splitters and amplitude transfer; now we are foliating not only classical events labeling them "in time" but also information: quantum phase. Then probabilities correspond to constant sections, while amplitudes (Q-states) correspond to "Dirac sections".

5. Quantum Splitters and Coproducts

A quantum splitter in the double slit experiment with equally spaced slits can be implemented as a coproduct:

$$SU_2: \quad \Delta Q = Q \otimes Q, \quad su_2: \quad q \otimes 1 + 1 \otimes q.$$

A quantum-amplitude-splitter/transfer can be implemented using the natural coproduct:

$$\Delta(n) = \sum_{n=p \cdot q} p \otimes q$$

achieving at the same time the quantization of the quantum phase via the *cyclotomic polynomials* (see also §7):

$$\Psi : \mathbf{Z} \to \mathbf{Z}[[h]], \quad \Psi_n(h) \ n^{th} \ cyclotomic \ polynomial.$$

This ought to "tie" the physics theory to Galois groups and Riemann surfaces, towards the "ultimate particle physics theory": number theory.

On the other hand, quantizing phase corresponds to quantizing time in view of the particle-wave correspondence and de Broglie "pilot-wave" picture.

In more precise terms, qubits are "rationalized" towards a "rational quantum theory". Correspondingly, a quantum gate should implement a "rational operation" (no continuum phase-gates!) processing quantum "rational" information (rational complex numbers: the Hopf ring of Gauss integers).

This has an analog in classical computing: computers have a "clock", and a "basic frequency"; all processes have frequencies dividing this basic frequency ("time unit = g.c.d"). Correspondingly, in particle physics this will be tied to quantum mass and energy later.

From the point of view of implementation, phase-changing quantum gates which are now **quantized** (pure *amplitude rotations*, without transfer) form the **basis of** $\mathbf{Z}[[h]]$: $f(h) = h^n$.

6. What about Distance?

As we have briefly discussed earlier, there is no apriori difference between space and time, except when deciding to introduce a space-time coordinate system.

The above quantization of time corresponds to a quantization of distance with universal conversion constant c.

If the above to distances to the slit are not equal, then a *quantum time delay gate* will act as a change in the distance "traveled" on one path, *compared* to the distance "traveled" on the other path. Distance is therefore **not** an absolute concept, and the "quantum angle" must be invariant (the conformal class of a metric matters). More will be said when discussing the "mechanics' simplified concepts": distance and time $s = ct$ (no i needed: not coordinates!), energy and frequence $E = h\nu$, mass and momentum $p = mc$ etc.

7. *Mass* as a Galois index

Galois algebraic picture in the context of the QDR has an advantage to the geometric Kleinean picture: it centers on symmetry; and entropy being a measure of symmetry and mass-related, we hope to end up with a picture of particle physics where mass is an index. With the de Broglie pilot-wave idea, in an "all-quantized model", including mass, the index is sort of a "musical interval" [2].

Back to "reality", a quantum communication (circuit/gate) $f : I \to O$ (1-morphism) has a certain symmetry; it is not necessarily equivariant with respect to a fixed group, but a fixed group acts on quantum communications:

$$SU(2) \times SU(2) \quad \leftrightarrow \quad Q - interaction\ symmetries.$$

DEFINITION 7.1. The Galois group of a quantum communication with Q-circuit f is the set of intertwiners (g, h) such that $gf = fh$.

---

[2] Particle physics: the music theory of the unicortex :-)

In the categorical picture, conjugations can be interpreted as homotopies. So the diagonal which invaries f are thought of as homotopies (natural transformations). In general $SU(2) \times SU(2)$, i.e. $f \mapsto gfh^{-1}$, should be thought of as "linear fractional transformations" (Moebus), a subgroup of $SU(2,2)$ relative the symplectic metric on $C^2 \oplus \bar{C}^2$ (The connection with quantum gravity will be made later on).

Now in the vein of Klein's geometrization program, one can classify Q-circuits or elementary particles according to their Galois group of symmetries. A tower of "Galois extensions" has an index; is it in any way related to mass? What is $[SU(2) \times SU(2) : Stab(f)]$?

8. Isospin and Flavors: Galois Theory?

The relation with Galois theory (Riemann surfaces etc.) suggests exploring an algebraic interpretation of quarks as algebraic numbers. The 1st isospin u, d with its anti-quarks $\bar{u}, \bar{d}$ seems to correspond to the 6th roots of unity:

$$u\xi, \ d = \xi^2, \ \bar{u} = \xi^{-1}, \ \bar{d} = \xi^{-2}.$$

The correspondence is worth being investigated if we recall that the primary object is the Hopf ring $\mathbf{Z}$ and its quantizations $\mathbf{Z}[[h]]$ (Hopf ring deformations) containing polynomials as basic amplitude gates (RS as zeroes etc), viewed as a Hopf object, not as a "field" $\mathbf{Z}((h))$.

Quark transitions can be modeled by changing coefficients from $\mathbf{C}$ to $\mathbf{Q}$ (qubits):

$$Transition : Down \rightarrow Up \quad \leftrightarrow \quad (I)_+ : Q_d \rightarrow Q_u{}^3.$$

Then $Gal(\mathbf{Q}(\xi) : \mathbf{Q})$ should enter the picture (or rather its Hopf incarnation). Interaction vertices would be related with Galois transformations and extensions.

---

[3]"Cadenza" of particle physics!

At this point recall that there are reports of *penta-quarks* (particles constituted of 5 quarks). So $Q + +$ the language should be "prepared" to describe such combinations, and any other *even/odd* combinations of quarks and anti-quarks.

On the other hand, there is no apparent reason for having *only* three generations! And because of the huge mass differences within the same generation, it is natural to look for an alternative mechanism. Since more energy means better resolution, a natural working hypothesis is to associate generations with the *length of the extension* (QDR/Galois). Then, IF the homological dimension of the Galois theory of the basic Hopf ring is three, this should explain why there are only three generations.

Returning to mass, which should be discrete as everything else, the natural coproduct $\Delta n = \sum_{pq=n} p \otimes q$ represented should lead to "mass ratios" (mass formulas). With $p = h\lambda^{-1}$ in mind (and discrete Fourier transform), the world is (quantum) digital the same way music is. Recall that a basic Q-gate splitter besides the path-splitter is the amplitude transfer or frequency-splitter in a rational ratio: $k : l$ ("fraction" k/l), the same way a music interval is (RCFT).

9. Riemann Surfaces and Galois groups

So, from [5], $SL(2)$ are the symmetries of $su(2) = gl(SU(2))$, and corresponds under the "Hermitian formulation" of Minkowski world to Lorentz transformations. Now these are the Galois transformations of the extension $[\mathbf{C}(z) : \mathbf{C}]$:

$$Lorentz\ transformations = Gal(\mathbf{C}(z) : \mathbf{C}).$$

This is consistent with our picture; briefly said, polynomials, zeros and RS appear in connection with a one-qubit quantum information channel.

Restricting to the level of amplitudes ($\mathbf{C}$), the symmetries are $Aut(\mathbf{C}(z))$. Now in the Hopf object picture, which corresponds to "delooping" algebra from one object to multi-objects (quivers, categories etc.), this fractional transformations are really pairs:

$$T(z) = Az + B, S(z) = CZ + D, \quad M = TS^{-1}.$$

Under the categorical picture, viewed as a natural transformation:

$$Lorentz : S \to T, \quad M(L) = TS^{-1},$$

this is the conjugation map C of [**17**].

In the *Hermitian formulation*, this is the SL_2-transformation between two elementary qubits associated to different paths, interpreted as a *change of coordinate system* (boost or gravitational acceleration).

In conclusion, the 2-categorical picture "resolves" the role of Moebius transformations from the commutative world (classic) to the quantum world of representations of quivers (e.g. matrices/Heisenberg!). At the same time it suggests and explanation for the "projectivity" feature of quantum mechanics. As we shall see later, a way to bypass Hopf objects and *still* work in the classical framework of "fields"/ratios, is to pass to *projective geometry*. In fact, "fields" as moduli spaces of lines (double ring) (affine geometry) contain the initial object (ring) as **one chart** in the corresponding projective space; including the "other chart" based at the point at infinity restores the symmetric picture of bifields (Hopf objects), while **liniarizing the theory**. Instead of :

$$(Az + B)(CZ + D)^{-1} = M(z, 1)$$

extend to (z, z') (double) and linearize:

$$L(z, z') = (T(z, z'), S(z, z')) = (Az + Bz', Cz + Dz').$$

Then "decategorify":

$$\mathbf{M}(z, z') = Action(L(z, z')) = TS^{-1}(z, z').$$

When quotiening by "homotopies", the corresponding moduli space is the projective space; without a point it corresponds to the embedding $z \to (z, 1)$. Again, this is linearizing an affine geometry; the price to pay: projectivity.

CHAPTER 7

Motion and Interactions: the *Simplified Picture*

We will give in the next section the considerations which lead to a simplified picture of physics, accommodating both classical and quantum concepts.

Briefly said, "everything" is random teleportation with the speed of light (a meir convention needed to distinguish space from time once a STCS is in place), in the quantum fluctuating causal network. The average appears as "motion" with some finite ("group") speed less then the speed of light, yet with the heritage of quantum transitions: randomness leads to Heisenberg's uncertainty. Recall that Bohr's rule already is a corollary, as shown before.

We still present the steps taken towards to above stated conclusions in order to give the reader the opportunity to check: maybe we took the wrong turn at some point, and there is a better way ...

1. Mass or Energy / Particle or Wave - revisited

The "historical equations" in connection with quantum theory and relativity are: $E = h\nu$ (Planck), $p = h\lambda^{-1}$ (de Broglie), $E = mc^2$ (Einstein). The "missing principle" [28] is that "everything" is quantum information, and therefore quantized: qubits; under this discrete model (QDR etc.) the above "classical" equations gain additional "power", demanding a further unification.

Fundamental Principle 1. *All "particles" (qubits) are subject to a Brownian teleportation with the speed of light in the quantum fluctuating causal network ("graph" of the QDR). The classical quantities are derived as averages, e.g.* the *effective velocity and its momentum.*

Quantum fluctuations means inserting and collapsing subgraphs (subobjects). Teleportation can be thought of as a random motion in time also, forward and backward, with a predominance in the chosen direction with orientation consistent with the global orientation of the quantum communication (from source to target; see [8]).

In this way the particle-anti-particle distinction originates in the choice and use of a STCS; the picture is simpler without it!

What is light? It is an *elementary teleportation of QI* (finite anyway: it should start somewhere and end elsewhere in the network [1]).

That **there is only one speed** c, is a basic conceptual simplification of the model, consistent with the general idea of the DWT: everything is information; therefore "IT" should move as such.

The quantum network is a "complexified double" (complex category theory: PROPs) of the Shannon-Wiener decision tree (set theory). Now quantum entropy is a measure of the "branching" in space and "merging" in time: the flow of QI ("Panta Rei", remember!?) splits in "parallel paths" requiring larger quantum registers or merges into faster computations requiring higher frequencies. The discrete version of Schrodinger / Dirac equation is the Laplace equation with its variations (Hodge-de Rham Theory on QDR, Maurer-Cartan equation and deformation theory etc.).

---

[1]No infinities are allowed nor needed in this model!

In a quantum time unit of a Q-process, i.e. the period T corresponding to a certain "clock frequency" ν corresponding to an energy level $E = h\nu$, the *wave length* is:

$$\lambda = cT$$

Then the *effective momentum* is

$$m_{eff}c = p_{eff} = h\lambda^{-1}.$$

Equivalently, $m_{eff}c^2 = p_{eff}c = h\nu = E$, so that the effective momentum:

$$E^2/c^2 = (m_{eff}c)^2 = p_{eff}^2 = p_e^2 + p_i^2,$$

has two contributions from the external and respective internal "motion" (random teleportation).

Now c represents the conversion factor in the presence of a STCS (if one exists). But this requires to break the parallel-sequential symmetry (like a "Lagrange subspace") of the causal network.

Without using different units for the STCS, i.e. in "geometric units" where $c = 1$, then the "only" difference between a space-like separation versus a time-like separation is the sign of the determinant of the corresponding Hermitean form (the infinitesimal generator of the unitary matrix). In a categorical picture, the "interaction-free-motion" of the qubit ((1,1)-gate) is of the form $U = Q_{Out}Q_{In}^{-1}$ (see evaluating morphisms, above). Then this is the evaluation of the $SU(2) \times SU(2)$ pair of norm (squared) $||Q_{Out}||^2 - ||Q_{In}||^2$ when viewed as an element of $SU(2,2)$. This enables the distinction between "time-length" as opposed to "space-volume/length".

A qubit processed by an elementary Q-gate corresponds to a cycle/period T. The phase difference corresponds to the difference in distance along the two paths.

2. The Wave-Particle Interpretation of Qubits

The Q-gate is a 2-morphism capturing both the path and amplitude splitting:

$$Source \underset{Qubit\_path2}{\overset{Qubit\_path1}{\xrightleftharpoons{SL_2 \Downarrow Lorentz}}} Target.$$

with infinitesimal length a "Minkowski space-time interval" and "width" a Lorentz transformation.

Now a qubit has two useful *qubit representations*. The first relates the qubit with $SU(2)$ and the *Hopf fibration*:

$$Q = \cos t \; e^{i\theta_Y}|Y> + \sin t \; e^{i\theta_N} \quad (Spinor).$$

The 2nd relates the qubit to the Minkowski world via the Hermitean formulation:

$$Q = \cos\phi + \mathbf{I} \cdot \mathbf{K} \sin\phi \quad (Quaternion).$$

This second representation prompts for a correspondence with the particle-wave duality: $\cos\phi$ encodes the square-root of the probability (particle point of view) and the unit normal $\mathbf{K}$ the "wave vector" (pilot-wave interpretation).

3. Motion and Mass

To assimilate classical mechanics while eliminating the need for an "ambient space-time" we have modeled "motion" (deterministic and random walk) as *random teleportation*. This brought a huge simplification: "everything" moves at the speed of light; and indeed since "everything" *is* information (qubits), this is only natural. This is a generalization of Einstein's principle of the constance of the speed of light, which is again natural: not only electro-magnetism "flows" according to Maxwell's equations at the speed of light, but when including quantum theory, and yielding QFT, "everything" flows according to Maxwell-Hodge-de Rham-Dirac algebraic equations (Quantum circuits [33]) with the speed of light.

Then the fact that motion occurs with a speed less or equal to the speed of light is no longer a "limitation"; it is a direct consequence. Observed "mass" and "speed" are *effective quantities*.

Now "at rest" no longer means "stillness/immobility", but it is a "background teleportation" with the speed of light which *on average* proceeds in the general direction of the "ambient" quantum computation, but "getting nowhere space-like"; unless of course we change the coordinate system (perform an amplitude transfer via an SL_2 2-morphism).

This permanent background teleportation with the speed of light should be related to the Heisenberg uncertainty relations and quantization. It should also entail the "diffusion of information" as in any *random walk*, i.e. the spread of the wave function, which for small speeds is modeled by Schrodinger's equation (or Heisenberg's equation in matrix/Markov transition form).

The parameter for diffusion, corresponding to the transition amplitude (see discrete methods to solve the wave equation) should be the mass:

$$p_{int} = m_0 c.$$

Now mass should be related to entropy as a measure of entropy, and also to the norm of the internal momentum (e.g. quarks) the analog of the external momentum (e.g. electron) under the space-time Wick supersymmetry.

Brownian motion at "average rest" should be compared with an oscillation corresponding to the de Broglie pilot wave:

$$p_{ext} = 0, \ p = p_{int}, \quad p = h\lambda^{-1}.$$

In this Brownian teleportation picture the period can be compared with the *killing-time* and correspondingly the wave-length.

A *photon* is the classical information exchanged in the teleportation of the quantum state.

In the simplified picture we have:

$$ET = h, \quad E = pc, \quad p = h/(cT), \quad p^2 = p_{ext}^2 + p_{int}^2.$$

The "position imprecision" is a multiple of cT, greater then cT, so:

$$\Delta q \cdot \Delta p = n(cT) \cdot h/(cT) = nh \geq h.$$

Then Heisenberg uncertainty principle would also be a consequence of the *Fundamental Axiom 1* of the QDR-model.

Now, in the simplified picture of QID, if no STCS is needed, then c could be eliminated towards a simplified *Noetherian description*.

As said before, c is universal because of the redundancy in the STCS description which distinguishes between space and time. Only when translating from QID in classical terms and choosing a STCS, c is needed as a conversion between the three space-like branching dimensions of the parallel factorization of the computation, and the *effective* time-like dimension corresponding to the branching dimensions of the sequential factorization of the quantum computation.

Now internal momentum could be related to the loop momentum (quantum feedback in time) as in the Kirchoff's Laws / Maxwell's methods; there may be zero electromotive sources and still a solution with non-zero internal currents.

The dynamic equation of QID is essentially the Laplace equation, in the discrete simple model of flow on graphs, or in its abstract form of Hodge-de Rham-Dirac form (harmonic forms and decomposition [33]). Then the mass of a Q-circuit could be:

$$p_e = 0, \ m_0^2 = (E/c^2)^2 = p_i^2/c^2 = 1/c^2 \sum_{[l] \in H_1(\Gamma)} p(l)^2.$$

Now $p(l) = \hbar \omega(l)/c$, where ω, the "de Broglie angular frequency" should be a *harmonic cocycle*:

$$\omega \in Harm(\Gamma) \cong H^1(\Gamma).$$

It characterizes the *resonances of the quantum circuit*.

In conclusion, "in geometric units, particle physics is number theory".

Now a classical measurement extracts classical information, so it should perturb the state of the quantum system. Details will be given when analyzing the *quantum erasure* experiment.

In the quantum network description, "position" is not a fundamental concept, and the "distance", or rather the wave-length, is the relevant conjugate variable to momentum, which in turn is the *Minkowski form* of the *generator of the qubit*, in the *Hermitean formulation*:

$$p \cdot \lambda = h.$$

4. Quantum Gravity

In the Q++ implementation of DWT all is quantized from the start: energy and matter, symmetry and entropy, even the quantum phase. Then where is "gravity"? As suggested before, in this simplified picture (all is teleportation at the speed of light), gravity appears once we adopt Einstein's Equivalence Principle between inertial mass and gravitational mass, under the following "disguise":

Fundamental Principle 2. *An SL_2 representation of a Feynman 2-morphism is a* Lorentzian change of coordinate system, *defining a* discrete acceleration [2]. *A gravitational gate is an SL_2-gate (not SU_2!).*

Note that in the Fundamental Axiom 2 SL_2 matrices are allowed. SU_2 is associated with "free motion" of quantum information, yet with the inevitable branching/diffusion and collapsing; classical probability is conserved.

But in the quantum world the number of particles can change, so probability "off shell" (in some sense) does not have to be conserved (the probability picture is a projective version of the energy picture - see [**24**] - both in an L_1-formulation). Now gravity is an *organizational principle*, like in Penrose's interpretation in connection with the collapse of the wave function in order to explain the measurement "paradox". We relate mass with entropy as a measure of symmetry, so gravitational mass or inertial alike, are related to symmetry and entropy.

We interpret an SL_2-gate as a *change of the "ratio" between sequential and parallel computing* affecting "probability" as a "geometric measure" of how many particles (counted space-like: probability density) enter versus the rate of frequency of the computation as a measure of the speed of the computation (counted time-like). In some sense it is a *conversion between classical probability* $P = |A|^2$ *and the quantum phase* $A = \cos t \; e^{i\omega}$ *under a complex transformation.* It is an incremental "acceleration" of the quantum computation:

$$QGG : \bullet \xrightarrow{Q_I} \bullet \xrightarrow{g \; Q_O} \bullet, \quad Q_O = T Q_I, \; T \in SL_2(C).$$

To compensate the change in probability (localization), the entropy should decrease, i.e. the symmetry of the

---

[2]No slopes; use differential forms!

system should increase:

$$\text{``Acceleration''} = [Aut(Q_O) : Aut(Q_I)].$$

Now instead of acceleration $dp/dt = F = ma$, we should think "change in the momentum without ratios", i.e. dp:

$$\Delta Q = Q_I^{-1}Q_0 = Q_I^{-1}TQ_I \quad (dQ = Q^{-1}TQ).$$

Since there is no speed gain anyways, the effective mass should change:

$$p = mc, \quad dp = cdm.$$

Now if mass is a Galois index $m = [SU(2) \times SU(2) : Aut(Q)]$, or when including QG $m_g = [SU(2,2) : Aut(Q)]$, since

$$[Aut(Q_O) : Aut(Q_I)] =$$
$$[SU(2,2) : Aut(Q_O)]/[SU(2,2) : Aut(Q_I)] = m_O/m_I,$$

at the infinitesimal level of energy-momentum or entropy $(H = \ln|Aut(Q)|)$:

$$\delta H = \ln[Aut(Q_O) : Aut(Q_I)] = \ln m_O - \ln m_I.$$

So the change in entropy due to the *gravitational source* (gate) T is $dH = d\ln m$ which should be related to the von Newman entropy $Tr(T \ln T)$ via the index of T [3].

The above suggestion implies that *entropy is the generator of mass*; rephrasing, *internal vector momentum* is the generator of symmetry, with corresponding measures: entropy and mass.

The change in probability should be interpreted as a "clustering"/change in relative distances; it appears as "acceleration". A "black hole" with one *external* DOF results when collapsing the subgraph representing the subsystem under the IE-duality. The connection with the black hole radiation laws will be investigate elsewhere.

Let us analyze an isolated 2-particle (qubits) system, in the spirit of Mach (one mass/gravity should be due

_____

[3]"$Tr(\ln T^T) = \ln|T^T| = \ln Stab(T)$".

to the mutual interaction/dynamics). Put two qubits on the two paths of a loop between two QGG:

$$g_1 \underset{Q_2}{\overset{Q_1}{\rightleftarrows}} \Downarrow \; g_2$$

As "time passes" (Feynman-Markov chain: *observation of the system!*) $Q_{n+1} = g_i Q_n$ should exhibit a periodical evolution: "rotation of one body around the other". Does this lead to the inverse square law? possibly, if we recall that *entropy and information resides on the boundary* (Holographic Theorem [**24**]). It should reflect the classical stable picture (2-body problem), if quantum fluctuations are not allowed.

The above QG model is consistent with the internal momentum flow mentioned earlier. QGG are then *sources of qubits* compensated by a change in the symmetry. Gravity counteracts the diffusion of information (thermal death etc.).

Other related questions can be raised once the implementation phase is completed [**33**]: What about antigravity? How to affect the balance of entropy and symmetry?

CHAPTER 8

The Homological Feynman Path Integral

The DWT implements the "automaton picture of reality" (modeling phenomena computationally) using the categorical language of Feynman Processes: representations of Feynman Categories. Without going into details (these are dg-coalgebra 2-PROPs) we focus on a fixed resolution degree, e.g. a Feynman graph, on which quantum information flows as a random teleportation. We prefer to keep the "specific" denomination of Feynman graph for the general case for clarity.

Mathematically we have a $SU(2)$-representation of the Feynman graph, i.e. the graph is colored with qubits. The 2-morphisms are $SL(2)$-transformations thought of as Lorentz transformations under the Minkowski formulation, corresponding to the spinorial, or rather "twistorial formulation" we call the *Hermitean formulation*.

Coloring the edges of the Feynman graph with qubits defines a *quantum information current*. It extends to a functor on the path category associated with the Feynman graph viewed as a quiver:

$$dQ : \mathcal{P}(\Gamma) \to SU(2).$$

It is an *action groupoid* as explained in [6] in connection with Klein's program.

The action is functorial and Stokes Theorem holds (think NC-currents):

$$Z(A, B) = \int_{Hom(A,B)} dQ = Q(B)Q(A)^{-1}.$$

The above integration (pairing) is the unique functorial extension of the Feynman rules, similar to the Turaev's functor on tangles etc.

The category is with unique factorization modulo homotopic moves leaving invariant the integral (descends on homology/homotopy). On a random path $\gamma : a \to b$ $(a, b$ vertices of $\Gamma)$ within the graph/network/factorization, $dQ(\gamma) = \prod dQ(\gamma_i)$ is multiplicative (functorial), which can be expressed at the infinitesimal level (Lie algebra $su(2)$) as a *Feynman Path Integral* for the random walk on the given interaction mode represented by Γ:

$$FPI(a, b) = \int_{\gamma \in Hom(a,b)} e^{iS(\gamma)}$$

where $iS = \ln dQ$.

LEMMA 0.1. *There is $Q(a)$ such that $FPI(a, b) = Q(b)Q(a)^{-1}$ called the **quantum potential** on the Q-circuit Γ.*

In other words the graph/network/RS etc. IS the causal structure (one "history" [37]) on which the FPI lives, and there is **no need of an "ambient space-time"** (see also [32]).

A Kirchoff Laws / Maxwell's methods on electric circuits represent the model for a Hodge-de Rham-Dirac Theory on the Hodge-de Rham QDR (NC/tensor formulation [33] should have CFT on RS as an example).

The bridge to the electric circuits sigma model formulation, which embeds RS into Minkowski space is the Hermitean formulation (su_2-generators as Minkowski displacements, SL_2-transformations as Lorentz coordinate changes / discrete momenta impulses etc.). At this point recall that $det(su_2) = (ct)^2 - x^2 - y^2 - z^2$ with its twistor spaces of $\pm$-determinant/space-time separation. The random teleportation/walk is at the speed of light, but the effective separation classifies pairs (a, b) into space-like or time-like separated.

DEFINITION 0.1. This defines the *relativistic causal cone* of a *Feynman qubit current / cochain.*

The connection with the *Min-Cut-Max-Flow Theorem* will be studied elsewhere [**31**]. We might ask why $det \ln Q$ appears above and not a trace, as in the von Newman formula for the entropy [1].

THEOREM 0.1. - **Conjecture.** *The* **commutative determinant is** *a Feynman Path Integral when viewing matrices as representations of the total graph/simplex/quiver* Δ_n $T(i \rightarrow j) = T_{ij}$, *and the signature of a permutation as the action-character for the natural Feynman rule* $sign(\pi) = e^{i\pi S(\pi)}$:

$$S(\pi) = deg(t_1...t_n) mod 2.$$

PROOF.

$$det(T : [n] \rightarrow [n]) = \sum_{\pi \in S_n} e^{i \ \pi S(\pi)} T(\gamma_\pi).$$

□

Incidentally this allows to generalize the determinant to the non-commutative case (compare with Gelfand-Retakh).

DEFINITION 0.2. The *Homological Feynman Path Integral* extends the commutative determinant (Grassmann calculus/commutative de Rham theory etc.).

Indeed, FPI is a graphical formulation of NC-universal differential forms and the bar construction, which establishes a bridge with Connes cyclic homology (integration, cycles etc.).

1. The Simplified Physics Picture

Returning to the simplified physics picture where everything is teleportation at the speed of light, mass is a

---

[1]If A Hermitean $det \ e^{iA} = e^{i \ trA}$.

conversion factor between the wave and particle parameters:

$$\mathbf{p} = mc\mathbf{k}, \quad \mathbf{k} = (x, y, z) \; unital, \quad ||\mathbf{p}|| = p = mc$$

and the quanta of momentum corresponds to a qubit represented as a quaternion (see §2):

$$Q = (\sin \phi, \; \mathbf{I} \cos \phi \; \mathbf{k}),$$

where a "classical phase shift" was introduced for convenience.

Then "mass and space are dual" in several ways, sine momentum is conjugate to position/distance, and also because of the IE-duality.

2. What's a Qubit Anyways?

Note that a qubit represented as a quaternion exhibits both the classical probability $P = \cos^2 \phi$ and the corresponding *generalized quantum amplitude*

$$A = \cos \phi \; (I k_x, J k_y, K k_z).$$

If a prefered spin direction is chosen so that say $k_z = 0$, then (k_x, k_y) corresponds to a *quantum phase in the direction of motion.*

Regarding energy and action in a qlick (quantum period of a process), we have the following relations

$$pT = m(cT) = m\lambda = h/c,$$

$$E = mc^2 = h/\lambda = h\nu.^2$$

The factor $\cos \phi$ has the role of a mixture between space-like information (probabilities) and time-like information (order) regarding the quantum computation. In the measurement "paradox" the "which-way information" is space-like; extracting it is a projection operation.

---

[2]Interpret in terms of channel capacity, from the point of view of the Min-Cut-Max-Flow Theorem.

The presence of both "Yes" and "No" in a qubit can naturally be interpreted as corresponding to a space-like split of a particle by a quantum-path-splitter (e.g. two slits), particle which takes both paths at the same time with corresponding amplitudes. The two "parts" of a particle undergoing a path-splitting by a QGPS (also a 2-morphism, but we will assume that all descriptions here are provided in the lab frame of reference), also distributes the which-way information as **entangled classical information**: if we measure the position and we know the particle went one way we also know its counterpart was "annihilated". This provides an analogy with the quantum entangled particle-antiparticle pair. Recall that being a particle or an anti-particle is dependent on the time-orientation of the particular STCS used to coordinatize a quantum computation/communication (Feynman QI-current) through a given causal structure (Feynman mode) [3]

2.1. Qubits and measurements. When we do not measure the which-way information, we obtain interference between the two **classical** particle-path (Yes) and particle-antipath (No) information, as opposed to only annihilation when a quantum particle encounters a corresponding quantum anti-particle.

If we measure the which-way information we "extract" the classical information as if the other classical path-information (NO) encounters its anti-particle-path, a sort of an annihilation process. It also can be thought of as a transfer (teleportation?) of classical information (see §1).

A measurement "collapses" the qubit, in the sense that it annihilates the independence of the two amplitudes; it aligns the two amplitudes under the interaction

---

[3]Relate to chiral currents, Noether picture and Fourier-Feynman transform.

exchange (creation/annihilation) between the observed qubit and the observer's qubit (Eavesdropping on a quantum communication).

2.2. What oscillates? or rather ... what not!?

If we have neutrino mixtures of generations (*neutrino oscillations*), mixtures of particle-antiparticles (tunneling and particle-anti-particle annihilation), meson K_0-mixtures etc., it is only natural to generalizes these superpositions to external observables, like paths etc. This is the reason for "upgrading" the coefficients from complex numbers $\mathbf{C}$ to quaternions/spins $SU_2(\mathbf{C})$ referred to as qubits, as a superposition of Yes and No.

Then classical information oscillates ($P = \cos^2 \phi$) and can be entangled (quantum erasure).

2.3. Time, entropy and anti-particles.

Now strictly speaking there are no intrinsic anti-particles; only when we orient time of a STCS associated to a QC, some qubits flow in the entropic direction of the computation (by definition from in-qubits to out-qubits), while other qubits "flow backward" (random walk and Hermitean duality of the tensor category).

This disposes of the matter-anti-matter "paradox". Everything is matter, which occasionally travels back in time. A "creation" of a e^+, e^- pair by the absorption of a target of a high-energy photon is ... a collision-reflection of an electron traveling back in time (an "edge of the network" which goes in opposite direction to our observation as a QC/communication).

3. Trees and Shannon-Wiener Entropy

Trees are a graphical representation of set theoretical concepts and counting (discrete measure theory). If trees are Z-trees (sets with coefficients in Z), binary trees $\mathbf{Z}_2$-trees, then the "$\mathbf{C}$-trees are the Riemann Surfaces (RS).

Shannon-Wiener information theory can be recast as *integer currents on trees*; allowing creation and annihilation (coproducts, i.e. Hopf objects), and changing coefficients to complex numbers yields the qubit flow on RS (Feynman QI-currents) [4]. We must include the antiholomorphic part, which probably corresponds to extending the coefficients to qubits.

View a tree as a random walk on a "vertical lattice", with source $A = \bullet$ the root and target $B = \{p, q\}$, where $p + q = 1$ meaning that we "collapsed" terminals corresponding to a two sets partition, and we are modeling the relative density $p = k/n$ (probability: projective picture etc.). The morphisms $Hom(A, B)$ are the paths from A to B (forests if $|A| > 1$). The *partition function* gives the weights:

$$Z(A, B) : Hom(A, B) \to [0, 1]$$

in our case with only two paths, p and q. It is normalized so $||Z(A, B)||_1 = 1$ (see also [24]).

It is natural to **double the picture** [5] and consider *probits* flowing down the tree, to prepare the formalism for qubits.

To pass to FPI on graphs (or other FC), think there is a random walk/flow on the graph/lattice/etc., which is represented by a colored tree, with repetitions.

The relation with SW-entropy was explained in [24]; the probability picture needs "de-projectivised", to an energy/number of particles (integer) flow picture [6]

The flow of electric current on graphs yields Kirchoff-Maxwell Theory (homological algebra formulation; **Z**-coefficients).

---

[4]What is von Newman entropy of a RS?

[5]Hopf objects, not fractions/probabilities.

[6]Free Lie algebras and statistics.

3.1. The probit picture of probability. It is better to group p and $q = 1 - p$ in a probit of trace one:

$$\rho = \begin{pmatrix} p & 0 \\ 0 & q \end{pmatrix}, \quad tr\rho = 1.$$

reflecting conservation of the probability current.

If the partition function (essentially the probability distribution) is

$$Z = (p_1, ..., p_n), \sum p_i = 1$$

then the n-paths ("quark lines") are represented by the n probits:

$$\rho_i = \begin{pmatrix} p_i & 0 \\ 0 & q_i \end{pmatrix}, \quad \sum_{i=1}^{n} tr(\rho_i) = n.$$

It is even better to introduce a coordinate system with origin the "stable equilibrium point": $Z = (1/n, ..., 1/n)$ and compute the entropy in terms of the displacement from the equilibrium (Morse coordinates):

$$p_i = 1/n + dp_i, \quad \sum_{1}^{n} dp_i = 0.$$

Then the *generating density matrix* is

$$X = \ln d\rho, \quad d\rho = diag[dp_1, ..., dp_n], \quad tr(d\rho) = 0$$

and the entropy should maximize the norm (see the least squares approximation method).

After the *geometric picture* conversion, a probit is a rotation:

$$p = \cos^2 \phi, q = \sin^2 \phi, R_\phi = \begin{pmatrix} \cos \phi & -\sin \phi \\ \sin \phi & \cos \phi \end{pmatrix} = e^{J\phi}.$$

The conservation of probability $p + q = 1$ amounts to $\det R_\phi = 1$, i.e. $R_p \in SO(2)$ [7].

---

[7]What is SW-entropy?

Now the Clifford half-angle formula gives:

$$R_\phi^2 = R_{2\phi} = \begin{pmatrix} p - q & -2\sqrt{pq} \\ -2\sqrt{pq} & p - q \end{pmatrix} =$$

$$\begin{pmatrix} 2dp & -2\sqrt{\frac{1}{4} - dp^2} \\ -2\sqrt{\frac{1}{4} - dp^2} & 2dp \end{pmatrix} \approx \begin{pmatrix} 2dp & 1 - \frac{dp^2}{2} \\ 1 - \frac{dp^2}{2} & 2dp \end{pmatrix},$$

where $p = 1/2 + dp$.

The change of coefficients to complex numbers and qubits would corresponds to quantum mechanics (geometric picture) and yield an interpretation of von Neumann entropy.

4. From Numbers to Elementary Particles

In statistics we count possibilities (conserved), while in QFT the number of particles is not conserved; they are just "observed subsystems" treated as one black-box circuit, so there is no reason for a conservation. The number of quarks is conserved IF we follow the quantum computation back and forth in the observer's global time. *Quark lines* obey the rules of a Hermitean category ($SU(3)$ and $\bar{SU}(3)$ are not isomorphic; $f\dagger = \bar{f}^*$ etc. [8]). This should entail CPT-Invariance Theorem on one hand, and mass formulas on the other.

4.1. Mass formulas. For example [10]

$$1/2(m_n + m_\xi) = 1/4(m_{\Lambda^0} + m_\Sigma)$$

translates into $1/2(udd+dss) = 1/4(3uds+dds)$. Assuming $m_d = m_u = I$ within the 1st generation and $m_s = II$ ($\times 4$), $2(4I + 2II) = 3(2I + II) + 2I + II$, which holds true.

---

[8]A chiral theory could correspond to left duality not equal to right duality $A^* \neq^* A$ (twists etc.).

The quadratic formulas should have an interpretation in the geometric picture, as opposed to the case of linear formulas (counting/measure theory: L_1-norm).

For example [10], p.68:

$$m_K^2 = 1/4(3m_n^2 + m_\pi^2) \tag{4.1}$$

translates into $(ds)^2 = 1/4[3(udd)^2 + (ud)^2]$ $(m_d = m_{\bar{d}}$ etc.), i.e. $4(I + II)^2 = 3(3I)^2 + (2I)^2$, or $4(I + II)^2 = (27 + 4)I^2$:

$$(2II)^2 + 4I(2II) - 27I^2 = 0,$$

from which one can derive a *mass index*:

$$2[II : I] = \sqrt{31} - 2 = \frac{31 - 4}{\sqrt{31} + 2} = 27/(2 + \sqrt{31}) \approx 3.6.$$

Now it is interesting to compare with the quark masses [41]):

	Isospin	Charge, Mass (MeV)
	$-1/2$	$+1/2$
I	$d : -1/3, 360$	$u : +2/3, 360$
II	$s : -1/3, 540$	$c : +2/3, 1500$
III	$b : -1/3, 5000$	$t : +2/3, 174000$

and stare at the

Fusion rules : $3 \times \bar{3} = 1 + 8, \quad 3 \times 3 \times 3 = 1 + 2 \cdot 8 + 10.$

The experimental index $[II : I]_{exp}$ is $3/2$ while the above mass formula gives $[II : I] \approx 3.6$. Note that $31 = 27 + 4 = (1 + 8 + 8 + 10) + 4$.

Recall that "quark color" was interpreted as an internal magnetic charge (Hodge-de Rham theory etc.) as a consequence of "tripling time". So here $SU(3)$ is the *color* $SU(3)$, since flavors correspond to generations. Now the

$SU(2)$ isospin symmetry holds only within the 1st generation, so we rather need a group with a Cayley diagram with six elements, a "consequence" of the fact that $2 \times 3 = 6$ space-time dimensions (if generations do not correspond to the resolution depth), i.e. to an $SU(3) \to G \to SU(2)$ extension $(SO(3) \otimes_R SU(2)?)$.

And since we do not have to forget antiparticles, in view of a hidden Galois theory, one could consider the first generation as roots of unity (Riemann surfaces):

$$\xi^6 - 1 = 0: \quad u = \xi = e^{i\pi/3}, d = e^{i2\pi/3} = u^2, \bar{u} = \xi^5, \bar{d} = \xi^4.$$

Now the circular (complex) charge θ is the color (quantized to a multiple of "white"$=2\pi$ as a topological index), with its real charge $Re = \pm 1/2$. Under the 2:1 $SU(2) : SO(3)$ cover map it is mapped to $\theta(u) = +2/3$, $\theta(d) = -1/3$ (clockwise) [9].

In our IE-symmetric picture, "rest mass" is related to entropy (some internal Galois structure), and therefore to *internal magnetic charge*: color!

4.2. Electric Charge and Hypercharge. Let us recall the relation between electric charge $Q = Ee^-$ in multiples of the electron's charge, the barion number B, the projection of the isospin I_3 and generation number. For the first generation:

$$E = I_3 + (B + S)/2 \quad (or\ E = (I_3 + B + I_3 + S + ...)/2.$$

Recall that $Y = B + S$ (and alike for charm, bottom, top etc.?) is called *hypercharge*. A more general formula including all the generations should be related to the S-matrix of the modular category and Verlinde formula.

To model quark color for which the symmetry is exact (not broken) associate the colors R, G, B to the standard basis in the space of pure quaternions I, J, K, i.e. to consider the three standard complex planes embedded

---

[9]Is the fractional electric charge a covering angle? Then a topological interpretation implies quantization of charge.

in the space of quaternions: $(1, I), (1, J), (1, K)$ (Hyper-Kahler structure). Then R, G, B and their anti-colors seems to form a "Hyper-Kahler spin structure" (I-spin, J-spin, K-spin), towards a representation theory of the corresponding Clifford algebra $Cl(4)$, rather then $SU(3)$:

$$SU(2) = Spin(3) = Cl(3)^*_+,$$

$$SU(2) \times SU(2) \cong Spin(4) = Cl(4)^*_+.$$

5. $SU(3)$ or $Spin(4)$?

At this point recall that the Pauli matrices are the "coxeter symmetries" (braidings) of the quantum world: $\sigma_1 = [0\ 1|1\ 0]$ is the transposition, $\sigma_2 = i[0\ -1|1\ 0]$ is a "diagonal rotation" ($i\times$ symplectic structure), both in the 2D-external plane of complex basis $\{e_1, e_2\}$ and in the 2D-internal plane $\mathbf{C}$, $\sigma_3 = [1\ 0|0\ -1]$ is the "Hilbert transform" (we prefer names to indices). Moreover Dirac's matrices may be represented as 2×2-matrices over quaternions:

$$Cl(4)_+ = H \oplus H, \quad HT \otimes Id, \ \mathcal{I} \otimes I, \ \mathcal{I} \otimes J, \ \mathcal{I} \otimes K,$$

where $\mathcal{I}$ is the complex structure on the first factor. These are the *complexified quaternions* $\mathbf{C} \otimes_R \mathbf{H}$ which contain $SU(3)$ (and $SU(\bar{3})$?) via $SO(3) \otimes_R \mathbf{C}$ ...

So, are the mesons ribbons (e.g. $d\bar{u}$), thought of as boundaries of Riemann surfaces representing quarks? (Related to Seifert surfaces and knots, skein relations etc.).

"Skein relations" which for the 1st generation is an exact $SU(2)$ symmetry corresponds above (tentatively) to 6th-roots of unity ($2 \times 3 = 6$ ...). Higher generations, should correspond to Galois extensions/towers/groups, and not to a breaking of $SU(2)$-symmetry. The depth in the resolution relates to Galois extensions via the long exact sequence in homology, so generations could be in fact related to ... derived functors!?.

6. Quark Masses and Mass Formulas

The three generations have new quantum numbers and corresponding conservation laws; but to count how many quarks of type s, c etc. seems kind of primitive: *strangeness S*, *charm C* etc.

For a later discussion we present the relative masses of the quarks:

Generation	Isospin		Relative Mass
	$-1/2$	$+1/2$	

$$I \qquad d \quad u \qquad 2 \xrightarrow{\times 1} 2$$
$$\downarrow \times 3/2 \qquad\qquad \downarrow \times 4..5 \; (3!?)$$
$$II \qquad s \quad c \qquad 3 \xrightarrow{\times 3} 8..10 \; (3^2?)$$
$$\downarrow \times 9 \qquad\qquad \downarrow \times \approx 120 = 5!$$
$$III \qquad b \quad t \qquad 27 \xrightarrow{\times \approx 35} 5 \cdot 7 \cdot 3^3.$$

returning to the quadratic mass formula 4.1 involving the d, u, s quarks, one may speculate why the mass indexes do not satisfy $2(3+1)^2 - (2 \cdot 3^2 + 2^2) = 1$ (... "a la Eddington" perhaps).

7. Generations and $S_3 \times S_3$

Nevertheless the generations should be related to the lattice of subgroups of the symmetry groups (e.g. $S_3 \times S_3$); in other words, classifying embeddings S_3 in $S_3 \times S_3$.

The masses of the "external charges" (electric fermions) [1]:

Generation	I	II	III
Quark "up"	1.4..4.5	1000..1400	174300 ± 5100
Quark "Down"	5..8.5	80..155	4000..4500
Lepton	e	μ	τ
Mass(MeV)	$0.5 \xrightarrow{\approx 200} 105$		$\xrightarrow{\approx 18} 1777.$

Note that the values differ from the other bibliographic source, notably $m_u \neq m_d$ even within the 1st generation:

$$u = \xi, \; d = \xi^2, \; 1 - u + d = 0 \;\leftrightarrow\; u - d = 1.$$

This means that the "product structure" $SU(2) \times Generation$ is not the answer, but rather a *long exact sequence* derived from a short exact sequence of complexes corresponding probably to the "internal-external" 2:1 IE-double cover:

$$0 \to \mathbf{Z}_2 \to SU(3) \to SO(3) \to 0$$

under cohomology (derived functors):

$$\text{"} 0 \to \mathbf{Z}_2 \to u \to d \xrightarrow{\delta} \mathbf{Z}_2 \to s \to c \xrightarrow{\delta} \mathbf{Z}_2 \to b \to t \to ...\text{"?}$$

$\mathbf{Z}_2, u, d$ etc. are only labels for objects to be determined later on.

An alternative to model generations is to view "elementary particles in the context", rather then "free + interactions", i.e. to view only the first generation in this way and the other generations as Q-circuits with their proper resonant frequencies:

$$R \leftrightarrow e < 1 : 2 > u/d, \quad LC \leftrightarrow II, \; III \;...$$

Another possibility is to view electric charge as the "white color" of **fractional charges**, in a confined **parton model of the electron**, as the only singlet [10].

Then the IE-picture would be symmetric:

$$Internal - External \; duality \leftrightarrow SU(2) \; 2 : 1 \; SO(3)$$

$$Internal \, Magnetic \, Charge \; 2 : 1 \; External \, Electric \, Charge$$

$$(q_u, q_d) \quad 2 : 1 \quad e.$$

One may ask if supraconductivity explained via Cooper pairs can be derived from a parton model and color of the electron, so that a Cooper pair, i.e. a pair of spin-up and spin-down electrons, plays the role of a leptonic-meson

---

[10]Fractional charges have been occasionally reported.

$e_u e_{\bar{d}}$. What is the exact relation between charge and color? (outer group etc.)

$$complex\ charge = exp(i\ color) \leftrightarrow S_3/Alt_3 = \mathbf{Z}_2.$$

$$White = 0,\ Black = \pi,\quad e^{iW\ or\ B} = \pm 1.$$

8. Mass and Symmetric Groups

The derived functors interpretation of generations is tempting, so we will speculate a bit more on the relation between mass and symmetry.

Entropy as a measure of symmetry $H = \ln Aut(\Gamma)$ seems to be the *generator of mass*

$$Mass = exp(Entropy) \leftrightarrow Mass = |Aut(Representation)|.$$

This is consistent with the mass-operators corresponding to representations of particles and mass formulas.

Now permutations S_3 pertain to the classical world and quantization often introduces $\sigma^2 \neq 1$; so a natural short exact sequence (s.e.s.) underlying the "big symmetry picture" SU_2/SO_3 is:

$$0 \to \mathbf{Z}_2 \to G \to S_3 \to 0.$$

S_3 is itself an :

$$0 \to \mathbf{Z}_3 = Alt(3) \to S_3 \to \mathbf{Z}_2 \to 0.$$

G (classical) should be related to the braid group B_n on n-strands (quantum).

There are too many coincidences above ($2 \times 3 = 6$), not to be a hidden way of interpreting generations as a long exact sequence in homology of $SU(3)/SU(2) \otimes SU(2)$ ...

9. Mass Formulas

Returning to mass formulas, we recall a few old facts regarding the mass operator.

The group $G = SU_2 \times SU_2$ yields the so called chiral algebras of charges; all states in a given representation have the same m^2 (F. J. Gilman/SLAC-PUB-323, 1967).

Gell-Man-Okubo mass formulas regard the irreducible representations of $SU_3 \times SU_3$; for example $M^2 = M_0^2 + M_8^2$ corresponding to the decomposition $3 \otimes \bar{3} = 1 + 8$ (A. Fernandez-Pacheco, SLAC-PUB-1922, 1977) and Wigner-Eckart Theorem:

$$< M^2 >= \begin{pmatrix} < 8|M^2|8 > & < 8|M^2|0 > \\ < 0|M^2|8 > & < 0|M^2|0 > \end{pmatrix} = \begin{pmatrix} O - D & E \\ E & S \end{pmatrix},$$

$$< 1|M^2|1 >= O + D, < 8|M^2|8 >= O - D,$$

$$< \frac{1}{2}|M^2|\frac{1}{2} >= O - 1/2D.$$

the quadratic relation 4.1 is obtained.

Mixing angles between mathematical and physical states are defined by (Clifford rotations?):

$$(\lambda_1, \lambda_2) = R_\theta(|8 >, |0 >),$$

where $\lambda :< u, d, ... >\rightarrow \mathbf{R}$ is related to the mass M^2 and satisfies:

$$\lambda[(u - d)^2] = 0^{11}.$$

The value $\theta = 10.9°$ is obtained (1977), which is $360°/33$. Now $(3 \times \bar{3})^{\otimes 2} = 1 \oplus 4 \cdot 8 + ... \approx 33 ...$

So SU_2 and SU_3 should belong to a "grand unifying group", may be $Spin(4)$, unless the unification requires a generalized cohomology theory.

10. Quarks and Cyclotomic Polynomials

Cyclotomic polynomials correspond to the *Universal Hopf object* $(\mathbf{Z}, \cdot, \Delta)$ (think $\hbar$ for X):

$$\Psi : \mathbf{Z} \to \mathbf{Z}[X], X^n - 1 = \prod_{d|n} \Psi_d(X),$$

---

[11]Universal forms.

i.e.
$$\Psi(\Delta n) = \sum_{p \cdot q = n} \Psi_p \otimes \Psi_q.$$

Recall that the "elementary particles" of $\mathbf{Z}$ are the prime numbers (generations-Lie dimensions), which are the primitive elements of $U = \mathbf{Z}$:

$$\Delta prime = prime \otimes 1 + 1 \otimes prime.$$

The Hopf ring $\mathbf{Z}$ is the UEA of the abelian Lie algebra of prime numbers, graded by the length of the factorization. The *Fundamental Theorem of Arithmetic* is the shadow of the structure theorem for cyclic groups (Fundamental Theorem of Abelian Groups), under the "logarithmic umbrella": Combinatorics is a Discrete Lie Theory!

If $\xi^n = 1$ is a primitive root of unity

$$Gal(\mathbf{Q}(\xi)) = U(n) \subset (\mathbf{Z}_n, \cdot), \quad [\mathbf{Q}(\xi) : \mathbf{Q}] = \phi(n)$$

where $\phi(n)$, the number of divisors of n is the length of Δn.

This Hopf algebra morphism is the bridge from Galois Theory to Riemann surfaces.

It supports the idea of a connection between quark generations (fundamental representation of G, maybe $Spin(4)$ with the "approximation" $SU(2) \otimes SU(3)$, or better of the infinite dimensional Lie algebra of prime numbers) and roots of unity ($u^6 = 1$ etc.) and Galois Theory:

$$(q\hbar - e)(q\hbar + e)(q\hbar - \omega e)(q\hbar - \omega^2 e)(q\hbar - \omega^4 e)(q\hbar - \omega^5 e) = 0^{12}$$

via derived functors (group extension: "symmetry braking").

11. Quarks and Prime Numbers

Since the entropy is the generator of mass, we should investigate the logarithms of the relative masses. After trying a 2-dimensional coordinate system $Isospin\ X +$

---

[12]A sort of a "Picasso-Escher" rendering of the idea :-)

Generation Y, as for a GUT group containing $SU(3)$ and $SU(2)$ (which still does not explain why 3 generations fully), we ended up with some "close-to integer-values, and the "Holonomy hypothesis": $\ln m_u/m_d$ and alike represents an index/holonomy about a pole close to the $u - d$ axis. Note that the mass index for the 1st generation is reversed.

Then came another "fine-print Evrika": what if the "elementary quarks" correspond to the Lie generators of the universal Hopf ring! (remember cyclic polynomials, poles and Riemann surfaces, the possibility that $u = \xi, d = \xi^2$ with $\xi^{2 \cdot 3} = 1$ etc.?).

The Holonomy Conjecture 1. The quarks form the Lie basis of primitive elements under the cyclotomic representation:

$$I(2,3),\ II(5,7),\ III(11,13), ... \overset{\Psi}{\mapsto} \mathbf{Z}[[\hbar]].$$

$$(11.1)$$

Their *Entropy* $= \ln Mass$ is the corresponding Galois index [13].

Now let's confront the above rough conjecture with the experimental data for the masses of quarks and leptons; note that the ratios are quite accommodating, but the conjecture is so beautiful, that it "must" be true: a candidate for *The Fundamental Theorem of Particle Physics!*

---

[13]RS: topological picture implies mass is quantized.

To start with, we compute the 2-d lattice ratio ranges [14].

$$I_3 = \tfrac{1}{2}(+\tfrac{2}{3})$$

$$u \xrightarrow{222..933} c \xrightarrow{121000..179000} t$$

$$Generation\ \#$$

$$1.1..5.6 \qquad 6.45..17.5 \qquad 37.55..44.75$$

$$I_3 = -\tfrac{1}{2}(-\tfrac{1}{3})$$

$$d \xrightarrow{9.4..31.0} s \xrightarrow{25.8..56.25} b$$

$$Generation/Lepton \qquad I/e \xrightarrow{205} II/\mu \xrightarrow{16.9} III/\tau$$

and their logarithms:

$$I_3 = \tfrac{1}{2}(+\tfrac{2}{3})$$

$$U \xrightarrow{5.4..6.84} C \xrightarrow{11.7..12.1} T$$

$$Generation\ \#$$

$$0.1..1.72 \qquad 1.86..2.86 \qquad 3.62..3.80$$

$$I_3 = -\tfrac{1}{2}(-\tfrac{1}{3})$$

$$D \xrightarrow{2.24..3.43} S \xrightarrow{3.25..4.03} B$$

$$Generation/Lepton \qquad \ln e \xrightarrow{5.3} \ln \mu \xrightarrow{2.8} \ln \tau$$

The holonomy pole is at $0 < \epsilon < 1/2$ in the generation direction, perhaps explaining the big difference for the lepton entropic index: $5.3 - 2.8 = 2.5$.

An integer approximation is plotted next to the value; since the primes are independent primitives, so the 2-d lattice distance is not a good approximation, we do not wary at this stage about the mismatch:

$$I_3 = \tfrac{1}{2}\ (E = +\tfrac{2}{3})$$

$$U = 2 \xrightarrow{+1\times 5} C = 7 \xrightarrow{+2\times 6} T = 13$$

$$+1 \qquad\qquad +2 \qquad\qquad +2$$

$$I_3 = -\tfrac{1}{2}\ (E = -\tfrac{1}{3})$$

$$D = 3 \xrightarrow{+1\times 2} S = 5 \xrightarrow{+2\times 3} B = 11$$

Here the "equality" refers to the cyclotomic representation.

---

[14]Maybe instead of isospin, we should use the fractional charge for the Y-axis.

What about the leptonic differences? And why the neutrino has such a small mass [15]?

---

[15]Maybe due to a large conversion constant between external momentum-mass and internal rest-mass (symmetry-information and Boltzmann's constant)?

CHAPTER 9

Q++ Examples

We sketched $Q++$ as a language to model Q-hardware (Q-circuits). Historically quantum programming was developed ahead of the corresponding hardware (quantum computers).

We will consider an important application, *quantum erasure*, to exemplify the process of modeling a quantum experimental setup (rather then a "quantum system" independent of observer), which we view mainly as a quantum information - classical information processing system.

The stages are familiar: decompose into elementary circuits, model the circuits as Q-gate etc.

For an elementary presentation of QE, see [16].

1. Quantum Erasure and Eavesdropping

As mentioned before §2, a simplifying assumption uses only one type of "particles", say electrons as carriers of quantum and classical information.

A source of electrons ("Alice") undergoes a 2-slit experiment observation ("Bob") under an electron-microscopy (em) 2nd observation ("Eve"), which "destroys" the interference (quantum information). If a lens is used to "totally blur" the em-image, so that Eve's eavesdropping fails, then this "restores" the quantum information content of the Alice-Bob quantum communication.

We will dwell on disassembling the Q-hardware, rather then explaining in detail the quantum information processing (copying QI, teleportation etc.) of this *eavesdropping process*.

2. The Quantum Erasure "Chip"

The Q-circuit has *sources* and *sinks* of QI and *gates* processing QI. For convenience the classical sources and sinks are treated as *input* and *output devices*, and modeled as "external legs" where only **classical information** can be read: *probits*.

There are several gates constituting the *QE-Chip*: the *quantum-path splitter* (QPS) of the double slit experiment, the *scattering gate*, and the *quantum-path merger* (lens) and finally the classical measurement gates.

Comparing our view with the current theories, we should emphasize that what is called "measuring quantum information", is a type of "interaction" which destroys the QI content ("collapses the wave function"); to "use" the QI one has to apply a different gate/protocol of processing QI, for example *teleportation* etc.

A second point refers to the underlying implementation of the *quantum software* which represents the formalization in $Q++$ of the interface of the physics application (here QE). The use of $Q++$ has made possible describing (programming) the application capable of computing what the real hardware will do when *running and experiment without the need to know the details of the implementation* obtained by **compiling** the Q++ code in a "low-level mathematics-physics code" (MP-code), for example QFT using Feynman Diagrams, or ST using Riemann Surfaces. The separation of the *application interface* from the *device dependent code* is crucial in nowadays complex knowledge systems.

Regarding the compilation of the Q++ code into MP-code the interaction gate can be implemented as a "vertex" in a Feynman Diagram of classical QFT, or a pointed Riemann surface in String Theory, except it will make the actual computations unnecessarily much harder!

2.1. The Double Slit. The double slit panel/wall has the role of a *quantum source*: a quantum-path splitter, also called a Δ-*gate*:

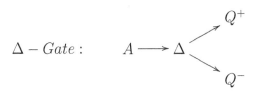

$$\Delta - Gate : \qquad A \longrightarrow \Delta \begin{array}{c} \nearrow Q^+ \\ \\ \searrow Q^- \end{array}$$

The *input* is a *classical source*: an emitter of non-coherent "particle-waves" (electrons, photons etc.). Non-coherence implies that it can be modeled as a source of :

$$\text{``}Current\text{''} \ I \leftrightarrow QI \ A = e^{i\theta},$$

("projective picture", similar to the probability flow on decision trees). The corresponding qubit is $Q = (A, 0)$, i.e. the particle-wave is "path localized" and behaves like a particle: "here? Yes=1 And No=0", i.e. its corresponding probit is $P = 1|Yes > +0|No >$.

The *output* is a **pair of qubits** (quantum register), balanced if we assume equal distances from the source to the two slits.

Now in the original two slit experiment the two qubits *interfere* into a *merger-superposition gate*. We will simplify the picture and "look" at the probability/particle count at a fixed spot instead of considering the classical interference panel/wall. The "two imaginary classical paths" are modeled as two *delaying wires*, which introduce a quantum phase shift if necessary. This can be alternatively incorporated in the QPS, but we prefer to list the elementary hardware components involved:

$$\text{``Resitence'' } R \leftrightarrow \text{'' } Distance = c \times Time \text{'' } e^{i\alpha}.$$

The merger gate is a *product* of the qubits:

$$Q_1 \searrow$$
$$\quad\quad\quad \cdot \longrightarrow Q = \{Q_1, Q_2\}$$
$$Q_2 \nearrow$$

It is followed by a reading operation (output) which extracts the associated probit:

$$Q \longrightarrow Q2P \ (Gate) \longrightarrow P.$$

This is the "wave function collapse" of the traditional quantum theories. While there is no natural place in a classical theory for this operation, and the various "explanations" limited to the "tools" available in the continuum quantum theory look overworked, it has a natural place in a Q++-program which **models information processing independent on hardware realizations**. Nevertheless a detailed QDR analysis should prove that such a micro-macro interaction/ communication produces the decoherence of the quantum information (quantum register) as suggested by the decoherence approach to the measurement "paradox", yet in a totally quantized/ discrete theory of finite type.

2.2. The Eavesdropping. The 2nd source is also classical (non-coherent electrons of the em), so it is also modeled by qubits-amplitudes E (from Eve).

Now the key point is that one of these qubits-amplitudes interacts with the **pair of the qubits**, i.e. with the quantum register in a *scattering gate* [1]:

$$I - QR \longrightarrow \text{S-Gate} \longrightarrow O - QR.$$

---

[1]The actual matrix which describes the operation of the control qubit on the input quantum register will be given elsewhere [**34**].

It is NOT correct to use classical logic and say that the "electron" from Eve scatters on the electron passing through one slit, **OR** it scatters on (the "same", unique!) electron but which passes through the other slit! The "real" quantum electron does is not always localized, and then "it" does not have "two" parts (cannot count quantum particles; only when modeling classically observed events [2]).

The two qubits Q^+ and Q^- are *path-entangled*, i.e. an external parameter/quantity pertaining to external space is "shared" by the two qubits, the same way an electron-positron pair "share" the spin property, as an internal space parameter/quantity (quantum observable; "observable" implies conversion to classical information).

When "localization" does not apply anymore, it leads to paradoxes to use a language or a model which assumes localization at its foundations.

Returning to the "hardware analysis" ("dissecting" a quantum IO-system), the output of the interaction is a *quantum register* (QR) consisting of two qubits (corresponding to the two paths), which are entangled not only in internal space, which leads to the usual interference when intercepted on a photographic plate, but also in external space, i.e. in terms of **classical information**, which can also **exhibit interference and teleportation**.

The detailed analysis involved in the Q-scattering gate is postponed for the moment.

Since we chose to measure in **two** (non-correlated=noncoherent) places/gates, counted with our classical logic (set theory), a vertex branching must be included as in an ordinary electric circuit, from which two "wires"/paths lead to the two measurement gates.

If the "eavesdropping" (control data: source and measurement) is not present, then the output probit from

---

[2]How small *one CAT* may be?

the 1st measurement Q2C-gate has the correct amplitude: the one predicted by the interference (constructive or destructive) due to the delaying corresponding to the differences in "distances".

Note that we not have to observe the "whole pattern of interference fringes" in order to assess the interference.

2.3. The Quantum Erasure. The 2nd measurement by Eve can be thought of as a "loop": Eve sends a probing QI and after scattering (Eve) observes the "modulation", i.e. how the interaction with the quantum communication changed the "carrier".

Now assume a magnetic lense is installed which focuses the two slits in one image. Such a lense "curves the space of paths", producing a *focal point*. This is similar to focal points of geodesics on Riemannian manifolds of GR.

What happens is an other reduction of the quantum register to a one qubit, under a *merger-superposition gate*.

The output goes into another Q2C-gate which again detects (or not) interference.

The main point is that the classical information *which-way information* can exhibit interference and teleportation. The measurement **at the focal point** (the lens can be permanently part of the experiment, while adjusting the position of the 2nd Q2C-gate in order to switch on/off the witch-way information content), will exhibit destructive interference of the classical information content of the 2-qubit quantum register, while a measurement elsewhere would exhibit a constructive interference, and hence the determination of the information needed to infer in classical terms "which path was taken".

This destroys the corresponding classical information (= external quantum information) at the other gate, due to the external entanglement of the two QR. The destroying process is also "collapsing the wave function", yet a **non-local one**. Since non-locality of QM is well accepted by now, it is only natural to "extend" the idea of "'wave collapsing" (Q2C-gates) from the "local theory" (at a localized measurement) to the general case of a non-local measurement. Nevertheless classical information, i.e. probits and bits are local. To "restore the interference" at Q2C1, we need the classical information from Q2C2. Now the only "restriction" still remains that "everything is teleportation at the speed of light", so this can be done with the speed of light.

Now is there a "true" *retrocausation* [3] involved?

No, it is not! The interference pattern (classical/external path-information) is "scrambled" by Eve's eavesdropping, and restored if Eve makes the corresponding information available to Bob.

2.4. Quantum registers or paths? The above interaction gate is not an "irreducible gate". It can be decomposed into two identical gates operating on one qubit under the control amplitude from the second classical source (CS2): This is analogous to a transistor and perhaps as important as well!

Then the quantum register is no longer needed, since only qubits flow through wires, except now we have to introduce two wires and a merger vertex before the two measurement gates, which will replace the superposition gate (Q-add/conjunction).

3. Q++: Modeling from Micro to Macro

The above examples showed how to model (program) the interface of the *physics application*. The quantum

---

[3]I.e. without antiparticles present.

computing Q++ qubit-data/ gate picture/ language allows to design both the quantum software and quantum
hardware [**34**] [4].

On the other hand, the elementary particle level is
also included (different compiling level: "machine code"),
and there is no *apriori difference*, except from the tech-
nological point of view: we can easily realize quantum
erasure on our desks, but not quite so with the "other"
quantum circuits (and why not, really?). It is safe to
"play" with qubits (e.g. polarized light, grids etc.), but
not with quarks!

---

[4]There is no question whether "the theory" is true or false,
since it is a language capable to express quantum phenomena. On
the other hand there will always be "good and bad Q-programs",
Q-bugs etc..

CHAPTER 10

Epilog

The present version of the DWT sketches the "object-oriented" Q++ language and provides implementation considerations.

Q++ is similar in purpose and presentation to any other computer programming language (automaton/formal languages/logic correspondence), except the gates process quantum digits [1].

The mathematics tools/technology needed to take into account quantum fluctuations, i.e. a *dynamic hardware* as opposed to a fixed hardware configuration is encapsulated into the QDR approach.

Its *mathematical core* the *Homological Feynman Path Integral* (Feynman processes on dg-coalgebra 2-categories) with its *physical interface* as *Quantum Information Dynamics* on *Quantum Circuits* (*Non-commutative Hodge-de Rham-Dirac Theory on the Quantum Dot Resolution*), provides an "all-quantized-no-renormalization-needed" model of quantum information flow: random teleportation at the speed of light, the theoretical basis for *non-conventional transportation methods*.

There is no apriori space nor time or distance; we only model (eavesdropping) on a quantum communication through a quantum communication channel.

---

[1]Computational details will appear in [**34**].

Our In-Out natural orientation makes us "see" only matter, most of the time. The random teleportation involves occasional random walk back in time we call "antimatter"; viewed in this way, it is retrocausation!

The model interprets *entropy as the generator of mass*, which is a *measure of symmetry*. There is *only one particle*, the qubit, with dual functions: data and gate. The "rest" is achieved by the *Internal-External duality* which accounts for the missing energy and momentum from external space ("neutrino"), the 2:1 correspondence between the basic quark-pair (u, d) and lepton (e), with generations implemented later on as derived functors of the same 2:1 fundamental short exact sequence.

The doubling in the quantization process of current theories steams from the completion approach in the commutative world: fields of fractions (and then real numbers: Newton-Leibnitz space-time and analysis!). The "shortcut" is *Hopf Theory*!

Finally, quantum gravity is an organizational principle: organizing the quantum information sources and flow to minimize/optimize the "quantum thought" (Lorentz transformation as a 2-morphism to maximize/symmetrize the qubit flow).

In the literature, the universe is often compared with a quantum computer. May be it deserves more; it is a *cognitive system*, and we are just "half of the picture". Observing and modeling our exterior coincides with its organization (cooling: lowering the entropy), not destined for a "thermal death", and acquiring an entropic arrow for the "US-IT" permanent communication. Let's not forget that we are not just "individuals"; we are connected in many ways we are only starting to explore ...

Is the *Digital World Theory* "Science or Fiction"? It is a consistent scientific project in the design phase (not fully computational yet), with important conceptual and practical implications in the near future.

"Ultimate Particle Physics Theory" is Number Theory *as the balance between the algebraic interpretation* (Galois Theory) *and geometric interpretation* (Klein's Program).

On the other hand (rather "hemisphere") we should keep the real big picture:

Reality *is* "The Quantum Matrix"!

"Everything" is quantum information flow, with its discrete quantum branching on rational Riemann surfaces as Pythagorean chords

"The Quantum Music of the Unicortex"

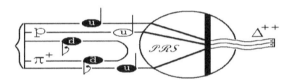

Its qubits tell the never-ending story of the life cycle.

To be and not to be, this is the answer!

said *The Cat In The Box* emphatically and ...

The End

Acknowledgments

The list of people I am in debt for useful discussions is too long to include it here.

I need to thank D. Ghitescu, G. Andreescu for stimulating discussions and their continuous moral support.

Bibliography

[1] S. A. Abel and C. Munoz, Quark and lepton masses and mixing angles from superstring constructions, jhep022003010.pdf.

[2] F. Akman and L. M. Ionescu, A Survey of Huebschmann and Stasheff's Paper: Formal solution of the master equation via HPT and deformation theory, arXiv:0704.0432; to appear in Int. J. Pure and Applied Mathematics, 2007.

[3] F. Akman, L. M. Ionescu and P. A. Sissokho, On deformation theory and graph homology, J. Algebra Vol. 310/2 (2007), pp.730-741; math.QA/0507077.

[4] A. Beliakova, geometric construction of spinors in modular categories, Algebraic and Geometric Topology, Vol 3(2003), 969-992.

[5] J. Baez, math.ucr.edu/home/baez/week201.

[6] J. Baez, math.ucr.edu/home/baez/week249.

[7] B. Bakalov and A. Kirillov, Lectures on tensor categories and modular functors, University Lecture Series, AMS 2000.

[8] B. Coecke, Quantum information-flow, concretely, and axiomatically, quant-ph/0506132.

[9] B. Coecke, Kindergarten quantum mechanics, quant-ph/0510032.

[10] C. D. Coughlan, J. E. Dodd and B. M. Gripaios, The Ideas of Particle Physics, 3rd ed., Cambridge University Press, 2006.

[11] D. Fiorenza and L. M. Ionescu, Graph complexes in deformation quantization, Lett. Math. Phys., Vol. 73, No.3, September 2005, p.193-208; math.QA/0505410.

[12] S. I. Gelfand and Yu. I. Manin, Homological algebra, Springer, 1999.

[13] M. B. Green, J. H. Schwartz and E. witten, Superstring theory, Cambridge university Press, 2005.

[14] H. Hammer, Shannon-Wiener information and trees, Trends in Quantum Physics, V. Krasnoholovets and F. Columbus (editors), Nova Science Publishers, Inc., 2004.

[15] A. J. Hanson, Visualizing quaternions, 2006.

[16] R. Hillmer and P. Kwiat, A Do-It-Yourself Quantum Erasure, Scientific American, May 2007.

[17] L. M. Ionescu, Categorification and Group Extensions, Appl. Cat. Str. 10 (2002), 35-47; math.CT/9906038, 1999.

[18] L. M. Ionescu, Remarks on quantum theory and noncommutative geometry, Int. J. Pure and Applied Math., Vol.11, No.4, 2004, pp.363-376.; math/0006024, 2000.

[19] L. M. Ionescu, Perturbative Quantum Field Theory and Configuration integrals, hep-th/0307062, 2003.

[20] L. M. Ionescu, M. Marsalli, A Hopf algebra deformation approach to renormalization, hep-th/ 0307112, 2003.

[21] L. M. Ionescu, Perturbative Quantum Field Theory and L_∞-Algebras, Advances in Topological Quantum Field Theory, Proceedings of the NATO ARW on New Techniques in Topological Quantum Field Theory, editor J. Bryden, Kluwer Academic Publishers, 2004, p. 243-252.

[22] L. M. Ionescu, Cohomology of Feynman graphs and perturbative Quantum Field Theory, Focus on Quantum Field Theory, Nova Publishers Inc., O. Kovras (editor), ISBN: 1-59454-126-4, 2004, 17 pages; math.QA/0506142

[23] L. M. Ionescu, The search for a new unifying principle, http://www.virequest.com/VIReQuest_UP.htm, 2005.

[24] L. M. Ionescu, The Digital World Theory v.1: An Invitation!, Olimp Press, ISBN: 973-7744-39-x, 225p., 2006.

[25] L. M. Ionescu, The Feynman Legacy, math.QA/0701069, 2007.

[26] L. M. Ionescu, From operads and PROPs to Feynman processes, JP Alg. Number Theory and Applications, 2007; math.QA/0701299, 2007.

[27] L. M. Ionescu, Remarks on deformation theory and quantization, arXiv:0704.2213, 2007.

[28] L. M. Ionescu, The search for a new equivalence principle, Scientific Journal International, Journal of Physical Sciences, Vol.1, No.1, 2007, pp.1-12; arXiv:0705.1116v1.

[29] L. M. Ionescu, Other projects and grant proposals, http://www.virequest.com/ISUP/VI_ISU-GP.html

[30] L. M. Ionescu, ISU seminar notes, http://www.ilstu.edu/~lmiones/.

[31] L. M. Ionescu, On quantum space, time and gravity, to appear 2007.

[32] L. M. Ionescu, String Theory: pros and cons, to appear, 2007.

[33] L. M. Ionescu, Hodge-de Rham-Dirac theory on the quantum dot resolution, to appear 2008.

[34] L. M. Ionescu, Quantum Informatics for College Students, to appear 2008.

[35] M. Kontsevich, Deformation quantization of Poisson manifolds, I, q-alg/9709040.

[36] A. V. Levichev, Mathematical foundations and physical applications of Chronometry, *Semigroups in Algebra, Geometry, and Analysis*, Eds. J. Hilgert, K. Hofmann, and J. Lawson, de Gryuter Expositions in Mathematics, Berlin 1995, viii+368 pp; 77-103.

[37] S. Loyd, A theory of quantum gravity based on quantum computation, quant-ph/0501135.

[38] B. O'Neil, Semi-Riemannian geometry. With applications to relativity, Pure and Applied Mathematics, 103.

[39] C. Rovelli, Quantum gravity, 2004.

[40] J. Vaz Jr., Clifford Algebras And Witten's Monopole Equations, *Geometry, Topology And Physics*, Vol. 1, Walter de Gruyter & Co., Pags 276-300, Berlin, Alemanha, (1998).

[41] Quarks, hyperphysics.phy-astr.gsu.edu/hbase/particles/quark.html

For additional references, by no means comprehensive, see the bibliography within the authors publications, esspecially [**24**].

Index